# THE Therapeutic Corporation

Studies on Law and Social Control
Donald Black, Series Editor


*Authority without Power*
Law and the Japanese Paradox
John Owen Haley

*The Therapeutic Corporation*
James Tucker

# THE Therapeutic Corporation

JAMES TUCKER

New York     Oxford

Oxford University Press

1999

Oxford University Press

Oxford    New York
Athens    Auckland    Bangkok    Bogotá    Buenos Aires    Calcutta
Cape Town    Chennai    Dar es Salaam    Delhi    Florence    Hong Kong    Istanbul
Karachi    Kuala Lumpur    Madrid    Melbourne    Mexico City    Mumbai
Nairobi    Paris    São Paulo    Singapore    Taipei    Tokyo    Toronto    Warsaw

and associated companies in
Berlin    Ibadan

Published by Oxford University Press, Inc.
198 Madison Avenue, New York, New York 10016

Oxford is a registered trademark of Oxford University Press.

Library of Congress Cataloging-in-Publication Data
Tucker, James.
The therapeutic corporation / by James Tucker.
p.    cm. — (Studies on law and social control)
Includes bibliographical references and index.
ISBN 0-19-511175-3
1. Conflict management.    2. Industrial management.
3. Industrial sociology.    I. Title.    II. Series.
HD42 .T83    1999
658.4'053—dc21        98-35069

9 8 7 6 5 4 3 2 1

Printed in the United States of America
on acid-free paper

To Erana

# Preface

How is conflict handled in organizations that greatly reduce bureaucratic authority? This book provides an unexpected answer. Conflict in such organizations is often handled through therapy, a form of social control not normally thought to occur in the workplace. Support for this claim comes mainly from an in-depth investigation of life inside an employee-owned manufacturing corporation (which I refer to as HelpCo) where people are relatively equal in status and socially close. I also draw on empirical material from other settings, including those with social environments similar to HelpCo such as worker collectives, utopian communities, and Japanese corporations, and those where inequality and social distance are extreme such as slave plantations, serf estates, and early capitalist factories.

This book utilizes Donald Black's paradigm of "pure sociology," a paradigm that has stimulated a growing body of research on conflict in a variety of settings. Much of this research addresses the social structure of law and other adversarial forms of social control. What little is known about therapy—the handling of self-conflict—comes from studies of psychiatry and other formal methods of treating of mental illness. But therapy appears under other circumstances as well. It occurs informally whenever people help others address what are considered to be conflicts with the self. As this book demonstrates, it can even occur in corporations if the conditions are right.

Some readers may regard therapy as more compassionate than other forms of social control. Others may consider it unduly intrusive or even morally deficient. In fact, much of the contemporary discourse on therapy, including scholarly literature on the topic, is evaluative, concerned with promoting or criticizing it. Yet the desirability of therapy is beyond the scope of science and is therefore not addressed in this book. My goal as a sociologist is to describe and explain this distinctive form of social control as it appears in organizational settings. The findings of my research do suggest, however, that the social conditions conducive to therapy are increasingly found in the modern world, meaning it is likely to expand into more areas of social life whether people like it or not.

*Portsmouth, New Hampshire*                                    J. T.
*July 1998*

# Acknowledgments

M ost important, I thank Donald Black, who provided valuable assistance at every stage of this
project. I continue to be inspired by his uncompromising commitment to a purely sociological science of social life and am
grateful for all of his help. I am indebted as well to three sociologists with whom I had limited direct contact, but whose
work influenced my own: M. P. Baumgartner, Allan Horwitz,
and Calvin Morrill. Also valuable were my numerous conversations over the past few years with Mark Cooney. Others I
would like to thank include the following individuals who commented on earlier drafts of this book or parts of it: Gib Akin,
Thomas Cushman, Michael Donnelly, John Herrmann, James
Davison Hunter, Paul Kingston, Stacie McCurnin, Jeffery Mullis, Roberta Senechal de la Roche, and Sarah Ryon.

The College of Liberal Arts and the Graduate School at the
University of New Hampshire provided summer financial assistance to work on the book. I am also thankful for the support
of my colleagues at the Department of Sociology at UNH. Finally, I thank Joan Bossert, Will Moore, Nirmala Darmarajah,
and others at Oxford University Press who were helpful at various stages of the publication process.

# Contents

# THE Therapeutic Corporation

# ONE

# Introduction

This book examines social control in postbureaucratic organizations—those without traditional forms of authority.[1] It applies a new sociological paradigm developed by Donald Black that explains social control with the location and direction of conflict in social space. An extensive study of an employee-owned manufacturing corporation combined with a broader review of workplaces, past and present, reveal that therapy—a form of social control that addresses conflict with the self (Black, 1992:40, 1995:835)—is quite common in postbureaucratic organizations. This finding may seem surprising. Therapy is assumed to be the domain of psychiatrists and other specialists trained in the treatment of mental illness. The modern corporation, usually characterized as a place where people are subject to an elaborate set of impersonal rules and regulations, would appear to be an unlikely setting for finding social control that responds sympathetically to deviant behavior and helps individuals overcome their perceived intrapersonal troubles. Yet, as Blackian theory predicts, therapy thrives on the social conditions that typify the postbureaucratic organization—equality, homogeneity, and intimacy.

Therapy contrasts sharply with the more authoritative and partisan forms of social control,[2] including violence, found in work settings with high levels of inequality and social distance. People subject to therapy frequently initiate and participate in the social control process, and individual circumstances rather than standardized procedures guide its application. Therapy is also distinguished by an absence of antagonism and condemnation. It does not proceed, however, by avoiding or displaying indifference toward others. To the contrary, therapy evaluates and attempts to normalize the self (Black, 1976:4, 1995:835; Horwitz, 1984:214), and in doing so is concerned not only with people's minds but their physiologies, social backgrounds, interpersonal relationships, and any other aspects of life thought to affect mental health.[3]

Therapy in the postbureaucratic organization flows down, across, and up the hierarchy. Individuals thus find themselves diagnosed and treated by their managers, peers, and even subordinates. Managers engage in the most formal and visible therapeutic strategies. They encourage individuals to help themselves, direct counseling sessions, and change people's surroundings by moving them to parts of the enterprise thought to be more compatible with their personalities and modifying the organization itself. Peers are more informal and subtle than managers when attempting to resolve self-conflicts. They accommodate each other as much as possible, but do not hesitate to express their feelings to coworkers, even if this means offending others. Managers also intervene as therapeutic mediators and attempt to reconcile differences between peers. Subordinates engage in therapy, too, by consulting with fellow employees, engaging in therapeutic gossip and disguising their attempts to help by changing their behavior toward managers. And superiors themselves regularly solicit advice from below on how to address their self-conflicts.

Later chapters explore further the behavior of therapy in organizations. Chapter 2 provides an introduction to HelpCo (a pseudonym), the organization featured in this book. In chapters 3 through 5, I present the findings and show how Blackian theory explains the handling of conflict (therapeutic and otherwise) down, across, and up the organizational hierarchy at HelpCo and elsewhere. Chapter 6 considers the broader significance of the *therapeutic corporation* and the extent to which it exhibits change occurring more generally in parts of modern society. This chapter sets the stage by first describing the radically new sociological paradigm developed by Donald Black. Next is a discussion of Black's theory of the third party, which includes an explanation of therapy. I then review the general characteristics of the postbureaucratic organization and the different patterns of therapy it produces.

## The Blackian Paradigm

Donald Black, in a series of books and articles published over the past quarter century, advances a new paradigm for the study of human behavior. The Blackian paradigm—called *pure sociology*[4]—represents a significant departure from conventional social science. Fundamentally, it provides a conceptual framework and theoretical strategy that operate at the purely social level. Consider first Black's new ontology of social life: Individual action is reconceptualized as social action. What is normally thought of as the behavior of persons or groups becomes the behavior of a particular form of social life. A woman calling the police and a corporation filing a lawsuit, for instance, are reconceptualized as law entering a social situation, or the behavior of law. A man hitting his spouse and a mob setting fire to a building are reconceptualized as violence entering a social situation, or the behavior of violence. A minister giving a sermon and a family going to church are reconceptualized as religion entering a social situation, or the behavior of religion. As Black notes: "The social universe contains countless forms of social life, and we can study all of their behavior in its own terms. In the history of scientific thought, this is a new subject matter—a new dependent variable, something new to explain, a new form of life" (1995:859).

How do we explain this new form of life? Black offers a theoretical strategy that, like his conceptual framework, is purely sociological. Social life is explained not by the motivations, feelings, interests, or goals of persons or groups, but by its location, direction, and distance in a multidimensional *social space*.[5] The dimensions of social space "incorporate and harness the explanatory power of diverse [sociological] theories and variables" (1995:851): Wealth and stratification are incorporated in the vertical dimension; intimacy,[6] interdependence, and integration in the horizontal dimension; culture in the symbolic dimension, organization in the corporate dimension; and social control in the normative dimension. To explain human behavior by using the Blackian paradigm is to show how it is situated along the various dimensions of social space, or in other words, to identify its *social structure*.[7]

The social structure of any instance of human behavior is defined by the social characteristics of all of the participants and the relations among them. How wealthy and stratified are they? Are they intimates or strangers? Are they interdependent? To what extent are they integrated in the larger social setting? Are they culturally similar to each another? How organized are they?[8] Some forms of social life occur only at higher elevations, among the wealthy, while others are found exclusively at the bottom, among the poor. Social life may also flow upward, from the poor to the wealthy, or it may flow downward. Intimacy attracts some forms of social life, but others thrive on relational distance. The location, direction, and distance of any instance of social life in cultural, organizational, and normative space also varies, and further define its social structure.

Black introduces the paradigm of pure sociology in *The Behavior of Law* (1976), where he presents dozens of formulations relating the quantity and style of legal behavior to various dimensions of social space. One formulation, for example, states that "downward law is greater than upward law" (21). It explains, among other things, why a lawsuit or criminal case is more likely to be initiated and be successful when plaintiffs or victims are wealthier than defendants than when defendants are wealthier than plaintiffs or victims. Another formulation, "law varies directly with relational distance,"[9] explains why lawsuits, convictions, compensatory payments, and prison sentences are more likely when adversaries are strangers than when they are intimates such as friends or family. Other formulations show how the quantity of legal behavior in any case or setting varies along other dimensions of vertical and horizontal space, as well as various dimensions of cultural, organizational, and normative space. Several formulations address the style of law. For instance, penal law, where offenders are punished for violating prohibitions, varies directly with the cultural distance between the parties (78), whereas compensatory law, where victims are compensated for their losses, is greatest in a direction toward more organization, such as when the accused is an organization and the victim an individual (98). The conciliatory and therapeutic styles of law, both of which are remedial rather than accusatory,[10] thrive among intimates (47–38). Explaining legal behavior from the Blackian perspective also requires knowledge about third parties: The social location of police officers, lawyers, judges, and any other parties who are aware of or involved in a case further defines its social structure and in turn predicts how much and what style of law it attracts (Black, 1989:8, 13–18).[11] Law declines and becomes more remedial, for instance, when legal officials are socially close to the adversaries (Black, 1976:44–45).

Black applies the paradigm of pure sociology to countless forms of social control beyond law.[12] He extends his formulations on legal behavior, for example, to etiquette, bureaucracy, the handling of conflict in science, the naming of witches in traditional societies, the treatment of mental illness, and social control in families and among children (1976:10, 31–36, 55–59, 80–83, 101–103, 118–121). Black (1983) shows how violence, while often attracting social control such as law, is itself frequently social control and can be understood and explained with his paradigm. He accordingly develops formulations on various modes of violent social control, including discipline (unilateral aggression against a subordinate), rebellion (unilateral aggression against a superior), and vengeance (unilateral aggression against an equal) (1990:43–49).[13] The body of Blackian theory also contains social structural models of negotiation (pursuit of a joint decision), avoidance (curtailment of interaction), compensation (payment from one party to another), toleration (inaction when a conflict might otherwise be handled), and much more (Black, 1987, 1990, 1993, 1995). Although mainly concerned with the handling of conflict, Black has applied his paradigm to other forms of social life as well, such as medicine, ideas, art, and religion (1979:156–161, 1995:856–858).

The Blackian paradigm has several advantages that make it

valuable scientifically. For one, it allows theory to be developed at an extremely high level of generality. Black's formulations thus order vastly more facts than other sociological theories. The theory of law, for example, "applies to all conflicts, civil and criminal, at all stages of the legal process, in all societies, in all historical periods, wherever law is found. It also applies to legal variation in entire communities and societies, including the evolutionary emergence of law itself" (Black, 1995:834). The theory of vengeance, to cite another example, explains diverse conduct such as Mediterranean blood feuds, gunfights in the American west, duels among the European nobility, gang violence in modern America, and international warfare (Black, 1990:44–47). Other Blackian formulations order findings from a comparable diversity of settings. Black has also reformulated some of his early theoretical statements and made them even more general. For example, he restates his formulation on law and relational distance "to apply to a vastly larger universe: the likelihood and degree of intervention by third parties of any kind, authoritative or partisan." The new, more general formulation reads: "Third-party intervention varies directly with relational distance" (1995:835).[14]

Another advantage of pure sociology, apart from its exceptionally high level of generality, is that its formulations are readily tested against the facts (Black, 1995:831–833, 841–846). Because it abandons subjectivity (thoughts and feelings) and teleology (goals and interests), theory generated from the Blackian paradigm can focus solely on observable aspects of human behavior. The amount of law attracted to any case, for instance, is directly measurable (Black, 1976:3–4, 1980). Were the police called? Was an arrest made? Was a defendant found guilty? How long was the sentence? Lawsuits, out-of-court settlements, judgments in civil trials, and other instances of legal behavior can also be counted and compared from one case to the next, from one setting to the next. So can other forms of social control, and other forms of social life. Likewise, the social structure of conflict or other form of social life—how much wealth the parties possess, the scope and length of their relationships, the similarity of their cultural practices, their degree of organization, and so on—can be observed and measured without imputing motives or speculating about how people feel.

The amount of evidence available to test Blackian theory is extensive. Black himself draws heavily on anthropological and historical materials, and is consequently able to show how his formulations order various empirical patterns in a wide range of societies and situations. Other social scientists are also testing and providing further empirical support for Blackian theory.

Black's formulations on conflict, for example, have been applied by others to topics as varied as homicide (Cooney, 1988, 1991, 1998), medical malpractice (Mullis, 1995), corporal punishment (Tucker and Ross, 1999), gossip (Herrmann, 1992), collective violence (Senechal de la Roche, 1996, 1997), employee theft (Tucker, 1989), and mental illness (Horwitz, 1982, 1984)— and to settings as diverse as colonial America (Baumgartner, 1978), modern suburbia (Baumgartner, 1988), executive suites (Morrill, 1989, 1992, 1995), day-care centers (Baumgartner, 1992), and international relations (Borg, 1992).

Applying the paradigm of pure sociology means ignoring the normal boundaries that separate areas of sociological inquiry. Consider the Blackian approach to conflict, a subject that includes an incredible diversity of human behavior. As Black notes, the handling of conflict is usually studied in disparate fields such as criminology, race and ethnic relations, the family, organizations, social movements, and religion (1998:xiii–xxii). Scholars in these fields and others are mostly unaware or unconcerned that much of what they study belongs to a larger family of social life that includes law, violence, mediation, avoidance, and so forth. Social scientists who specialize in the workplace, for example, frequently address conflict (see Black, 1998:xiii–xxii), whether regarding employer responses to employee misconduct such as absenteeism (e.g., Gersuny, 1973; Dalton and Mesch, 1990) and alcohol abuse (e.g., Weiss, 1986; Trice and Sonnenstuhl, 1990), informal dispute settlement among employees (e.g., Gwartney-Gibbs and Lach, 1991; Kolb and Bartunek, 1992), strikes and work slowdowns (e.g., Gouldner, 1954; Shorter and Tilly, 1974), nonunion grievance procedures (e.g., Ewing, 1989; Edelman, 1990), or covert methods of worker protest (e.g. Roy, 1952; Hodson, 1991; Paules, 1991; Jermier, Knights, and Lord, 1994). These behaviors, plus many others, have much in common with seemingly unrelated conduct such as lawsuits and homicide. But few of those who study workplace conflict, including organizational sociologists, industrial psychologists, labor historians, and management theorists, realize that it can be explained with a general theory that explains the handling of conflict wherever and whenever it occurs (but see Morrill, 1989, 1992, 1995; Tucker, 1989, 1993).[15]

Mental health specialists also study conduct that is often, upon close examination, the handling of conflict (Black, 1998: xiii–xxii). For example, behavior considered to be mental illness, such as depression, eating disorders, and drug abuse, can be an indirect means of expressing grievances against spouses, parents, or other intimates (Baumgartner, 1984:327–328, 1988: 30–36; Horwitz, 1990:41). Likewise, people who commit suicide—behavior frequently thought to reflect a mental breakdown—sometimes do so in response to abusive authority figures (Baumgartner, 1984:328–329; Horwitz, 1990:41). Suicide may also be "social control of the self," a method of punishing oneself for harming others (Black, 1992:40). And as Black demonstrates, a common *response* to mental illness—therapy—is also the handling of conflict, usually a form of third-party intervention (1995:835). Yet rather than address conflict between separate parties (adversaries), therapy deals with self-conflicts (Black, 1992:40, 1995:835). It attempts to help people resolve their internal or intrapersonal problems, to reunite the "divided self" (see Laing, 1960).[16] Disordered personalities, abnormal states of mind, and troubled souls are the kinds of afflictions that therapy defines and tries to cure (Horwitz, 1984:214, 1990: 81).

Although the focus of therapy is on people's psychologies, Blackian pure sociology of conflict can explain this form of social control as it explains others, by identifying its social structure.

## The Social Structure of Therapy

Black provides an explanation of therapy as part of his theory of third-party intervention. Therapy in its pure form is initiated when a party defines itself as deviant and seeks help returning to normality (Black, 1976:4–5; Horwitz, 1982:127).[17] It becomes a form of third-party intervention when a helper of some kind is involved in a self-conflict (Black, 1995:835). Third-party helpers are often skilled healers, and depending on the setting they may call upon supernatural spirits, analyze people's dreams, or simply listen to individuals talk about their problems (Black and Baumgartner, 1983:109–111). Whatever the particular type of help offered, therapy is a weak form of third-party intervention. It falls at the low end of the continuum of both *authoritativeness* and *partisanship*, the two variable dimensions of third-party intervention that Blackian theory addresses.

Authoritativeness includes the degree of formalism, decisiveness, coerciveness, and punitiveness (Black, 1993:145–149, 1995:834–835 n. 34). At one extreme are authoritative third parties who apply social control according to explicit standards, make clear distinctions between right and wrong, back decisions with force, and consider offenders enemies who must be punished. Judges are an example: They condemn people for violating rules. At the other extreme are nonauthoritative third parties whose intervention is characterized by informality, compromise, voluntariness, and helpfulness (Black, 1995:836). Mediation, where third parties help adversaries work out their differences without taking sides, is nonauthoritative. So is therapy (Black, 1995:835). In its weakest (or purest) form, a third party is solicited by an individual seeking assistance for an intrapersonal problem (Black, 1976:4–5). Therapists refrain from imposing cures. Instead, they help people find their own solutions. But therapy is not always pure (Black, 1976:5). Third parties may act more forcefully and try to convince people that they have self-conflicts. In state-socialist societies such as the People's Republic of China and the former Soviet Union, for example, individuals subject to therapy are usually pressured by others to seek treatment, which often includes coercive efforts to reeducate "patients to conform to the dominant ideology" (Horwitz, 1984:230).[18] Therapy in these settings is also standardized, with little variation across cases (Horwitz, 1984: 228–231). Therapeutic treatment can take on even more authoritative (and thus less pure) forms. Patients may be forced to take psychoactive drugs, for instance, or be subject to electric-shock treatment (Fireside, 1979). Surgical procedures such as a frontal lobotomy may also be used to treat self-conflicts (Scull, 1989:25,278).[19]

Partisanship, a second variable aspect of third-party intervention, refers to the degree of support a third party provides one of the adversaries against the other (Black, 1993:125–143, 1995:834–835 n. 34). At one extreme are what Black calls "strong partisans," who lend absolute support, often risking life and limb, to one side of a conflict (1993:131–132). They frequently escalate conflict. At the other extreme are nonpartisans. "Cold nonpartisans" are indifferent to conflict, often just "bystanders, leaving the adversaries to fend for themselves" (Black, 1993:134). "Warm nonpartisans," by contrast, are supportive, seeking to end conflicts and bring adversaries together (Black, 1993:135). Mediators and go-betweens are examples (Black, 1993:135). So are therapists, although they address intrapersonal rather than interpersonal conflict. Warm nonpartisanship thus overlaps weak authoritativeness, and therapy is both.

What determines why therapy rather than a more authoritative or partisan third-party intervention, will prevail in a particular social setting? Blackian theory states that the likelihood and degree of authoritative and partisan intervention by third parties depend on the relationship between the adversaries themselves *and* the relationship between third parties and the adversaries:

1. The likelihood and degree of authoritative and partisan intervention vary *directly* with the amount of inequality and social distance between adversaries (Black, 1995:834–837).

2. The likelihood and degree of authoritative and partisan intervention vary *directly* with the superiority and social remoteness of third parties (Black, 1995:834–837; see also Black and Baumgartner, 1983:113–114; Black, 1984:15–16, 1993:ch. 7–8).

The first formulation explains why therapy, rather than another form of third-party intervention, handles conflict with the self. Because self-conflicts contain the least amount of inequality and social distance (very little), they attract the least authoritative and least partisan form of third party intervention:

therapy (Black, 1995:835–836). However, the social structure of the self can vary. Self-intimacy, for example, increases when individuals spend more time with themselves (Black, 1995: 835–836 n. 37). According to the formulation, therapy should increase under these conditions. It apparently does. People who live alone, for instance, are more likely than those living with others to receive psychiatric care (Dinitz, Lefton, Angrist, and Pasamanick, 1961, cited in Black, 1976:119–120, 1995:836 n. 37). Moreover, in modern America, single people and those who are geographically mobile are the most frequent seekers of psychotherapeutic treatment (Horwitz, 1984:241).[20]

The second formulation predicts that therapy, as the weakest form of third-party intervention, is most likely to be applied by those who are equal and socially close. (Black, 1995:836). If we examine where therapy occurs, whether at public healing ceremonies in tribal societies or in the private offices of modern psychiatrists, we find that in fact it appears in its purest forms only when therapist and patient share a symbolic universe and are part of an ongoing relationship in which communication flows freely (Horwitz, 1984:216–217). Among preindustrial peoples, for instance, therapy is usually a collective affair; families and members of tight-knit communities work together to diagnose and treat the mentally ill (Horwitz, 1984:226). In the modern psychiatric relationship, closeness typically develops during the therapeutic process itself, which requires patients to meet with therapists for extended periods (see Black, 1995:836 n. 40).

The second formulation predicts other variations in the behavior of therapy. It explains, for example, why psychotherapy in modern societies is most popular among the middle and upper classes, who are similar in social rank and cultural orientation to professional therapists (Horwitz, 1990:84–86). Moreover, it explains why in contemporary America members of Chinese and Hispanic ethnic groups resist attempts by mostly white mental health professionals to provide therapeutic help (Garrison, 1977; Lin, Tardiff, Donetz, and Goresky, 1978, both cited in Horwitz, 1990:85).[21] If more distant and superior third parties become involved in self-conflicts, which the second formulation predicts to be uncommon, therapeutic intervention is predicted to be more authoritative, and thus less pure, than therapy flowing across shorter distances in social space. Evidence suggests this is so. For example, American mental hospitals became more custodial (like prisons) over the course of the nineteenth-century with the increase in the proportion of foreign-born patients, who were socially remote and mostly poor (Grob, 1973, cited in Horwitz, 1990:83). And in contemporary societies, lower-status mental patients are likely to be committed involuntarily, whereas higher-status patients are more apt to commit themselves voluntarily to mental hospitals (Linsky, 1970, cited in Horwitz, 1984:83).

The second formulation also explains why therapy takes on its most authoritative and least pure forms when initiated and processed by the state. Governments put people in institutions and asylums, restrict their freedom, and subject them to coercive therapies, often physical ones (see Goffman, 1961; Szasz, 1961). Because centralized governments are the most superior and socially distant from citizens (Black, 1995:151), they have the most state-run mental hospitals and the harshest forms of treatment (see Fireside, 1979). Therapy is also more formal when the government involves itself in the handling of self-conflicts. Mental disorders are named, psychiatric categories created, and patients classified and labeled (see Scheff, 1966).

To recapitulate, Blackian theory predicts that therapy, as the weakest form of authoritativeness and partisanship, is applied to self-conflicts and is most pure and most active when inequality and social distance are minimal, in other words, under the following conditions: *equality, homogeneity, and intimacy.*[22] Support for this formulation comes mainly from research on therapy provided by specialists trained in healing the self. This includes studies of psychiatrists and other professionals in modern societies as well as traditional healers in preindustrial societies (see generally, Horwitz, 1982, 1984, 1990: ch. 5).[23] Yet people with no training, special skills, or credentials may practice therapy informally. In fact, any time people trace the causes of deviant behavior to intrapersonal problems and respond in a helping manner they are engaging in therapy. Experts are not necessary for someone to be diagnosed and treated. Therapy is therefore found in many areas of contemporary life, including places where it might be least expected, such as families, friendships, schools, and even corporations.[24] Nonetheless, it obeys the same principles everywhere, and is thus attracted to any setting where individuals are equal, homogeneous, and intimate. One such setting is the postbureaucratic organization.

## The Postbureaucratic Organization

Organizations dominate the social landscape of modern societies. This feature of modernity has especially profound consequences for how people earn their livelihoods. For example, over 90 percent of working Americans make their living as employees in organizations (Fain, 1980:4, cited in Russell, 1985: 5). A long tradition of social science suggests that organizations, especially economic ones, are increasingly likely to resemble a bureaucracy (see Weber, 1925). The assumption is that the bureaucratic enterprise, with its well-defined hierarchy of authority, highly specialized division of labor, and impersonal network of professional relationships, is more efficient than other forms of organization. According to this view, bureaucracy should therefore come to dominate organizational life in the contemporary world.

Hierarchy, specialization, and impersonality are common features of many modern work settings. Yet some enterprises deliberately reduce their dependence on bureaucracy and incorporate democratic features. The former Yugoslavian government's attempt to run an entire economy on "self-management," whereby managers were elected and major enterprise decisions were subject to a referendum, was one of the most comprehensive experiments in workplace democracy (Adizes, 1971). The governments of Germany, France, Sweden, Norway, and Great Britain also promoted worker participation in the management of industrial organizations at various times in the twentieth century (Zwerdling, 1978). The Mondragon region of Spain relies heavily on locally run producer cooperatives (Whythe, 1988), and in Israel, many agricultural enterprises have decentralized communal social structures as part of the kibbutzim (Rayman, 1981). The oldest democratically run organizations in the United States include a group of about twenty plywood companies in the Pacific Northwest and several refuse-collecting enterprises in the San Francisco area (Russell, 1985). The 1960s and 1970s saw a growth in the number of employee-owned and managed worker collectives (Jackall and Levine, 1984). Some remain in operation, although most are very small and confined to the periphery of the economy in light manufacturing and retail trade (Rothschild and Whitt, 1986).

These enterprises are exceptional for the most part. The corporate world of today is hardly democratic. Managers are typically not elected by workers and executives usually have disproportionate influence over company affairs. Even so, a growing number of corporations are adopting a *postbureaucratic* organizational structure.[25] This pattern is especially evident in modern America, where firms in various industries have decentralized hierarchy, reduced specialization, and fostered the development of strong personal relationships among employees.

Decentralization takes on several forms. Most large Fortune 500 companies and many smaller firms have employee-participation programs that allow workers input in decisions affecting their jobs (Lawler, 1992). One such strategy delegates authority to groups of employees who manage themselves with little interference from superiors (Applebaum and Batt, 1994; Osterman, 1994). Inspired by Japanese "quality circles," this strategy was originally developed to encourage innovation among engineers in high-technology firms. In recent years, companies have also experimented with programs that give decision-making responsibility to teams of rank-and-file production workers (Heckscher and Applegate, 1994).[26] Corporations are also decentralizing ownership. For example, almost 10 percent of the American labor force works for companies that are at least partially owned by employees.[27] Ownership is often limited, meaning that employee influence over company matters is not necessarily substantial.[28] Nonetheless, these firms differ from conventional bureaucratic companies, where ownership is concentrated among top management or outside stockholders.

Specialization, a second bureaucratic attribute, has also been reduced in parts of corporate America. This is sometimes accomplished by abolishing job descriptions and titles or downplaying their importance (Kanter, 1989:282). Differentiation is also weakened when employees periodically change positions within a company. Often called "job rotation," this practice broadens employee work experience and eliminates the parochialism that often characterizes bureaucratic organizations (Ouchi, 1981:25–32). Interdepartmental activities such as task forces, training workshops, and company-sponsored athletic events further promote homogeneity in corporate settings (Kunda, 1992).

Another defining feature of bureaucracy is a strict separation of members' organizational and personal lives. This, too, has weakened in some work settings. Apart from evidence indicating such a separation is rarely achieved in practice, organizations that emphasize teamwork and cooperation find that close emotional relationships, including romantic ones, develop with regularity. Moreover, in contrast to the classic bureaucratic firm, people in some corporations are actively encouraged to display their emotions in forums such as meditation sessions and weekend retreats (Kanter, 1989:280–285).

In summary, the postbureaucratic organization is emerging as a distinct organizational type.[29] Relationships in this setting are more equal, homogenous, and intimate than in the traditional workplace. This is precisely the kind of setting where therapy flourishes.

### Therapy in Corporations

The following chapters describe when and how therapy involves itself in organizational life. Most of the empirical material comes from an in-depth study of social control at HelpCo, an employee-owned manufacturing corporation. The patterns of therapy found in this organization are also present in similarly structured settings such as communes, worker collectives, utopian communities, and Japanese businesses. They are present as well in conventional bureaucratic organizations containing pockets of equality, homogeneity, and intimacy.[30]

Therapy in the postbureaucratic organization is sometimes initiated when a party defines himself or herself as experiencing a self-conflict and in need of help. It may be an executive who believes he has a drinking problem, an accountant unhappy with her tendency to dwell on mistakes, or a production worker frustrated with his lack of drive. In most cases, however, therapy is initiated by those attempting to help. Individuals across the enterprise continually diagnose and treat fellow employees. Help is usually informal and often subtle, although the direction of therapy, whether downward, lateral, or upward, determines the precise forms it takes.

Therapy is most forceful and visible when directed downward, from superiors to subordinates. Managers attribute deviant behavior to personal characteristics or circumstances and encourage people to help themselves as much as possible. Subordinates may be convinced to talk about their problems in meetings that resemble psychiatric counseling sessions. Managers may also change the surroundings of those determined to be experiencing conflicts with themselves. Consider a typical case of managerial therapy at HelpCo. The case was activated when Tyler, an accountant, was repeatedly observed by Kyle, his team leader, to be "sluggish." After reflecting on the matter and discussing it with others, Kyle invited Tyler to lunch in an attempt to discover the source of the alleged self-conflict. Tyler was initially reluctant to share his thoughts, but eventually "opened up." Together the two parties determined that the problem stemmed from Tyler's "deep insecurities," which were highlighted with the recent hiring of Lance, a young accountant with an outgoing personality. Among other things, Tyler defined Lance as a threat to his long-standing popularity among other workers. Kyle explained to Tyler that he would ultimately have to "work things out on his own," but promised to have lunch with him every other week in order to make sure he is "dealing with the issues." At the same time, Lance was persuaded to move his office so that it was farther from Tyler's office. The hope was that this would give Tyler a chance to work on his problems without constantly coming into contact with Lance.

Lateral therapy is frequently combined with conciliation. Peers tend to accept others and what are defined as their unique personalities, but they also express themselves verbally in order to help themselves and others overcome their alleged intrapersonal problems. Supervisors may act as mediators, reconciling differences between peers and restoring harmony to relationships. A representative example of lateral therapy occurred in HelpCo's engineering department. This case commenced when Brad, an engineer, upset with himself for yelling at a fellow employee, left work in the middle of the day to go home and "cool down." The next morning he apologized to his coworker, Neil, but remained frustrated at the breakdown of communication. Jeff, their team leader, became aware of the tension developing between the two and brought them together on several occasions so they could "get to know each other's personalities." Both Brad and Neil came to define themselves as "fundamentally different people" and agreed to "work around their differences."

Therapy directed upward is the most covert. Subordinates secretly evaluate managers, often collectively, and disguise their attempts to help by adjusting their behavior in some way. Moreover, managers may turn to subordinates for assistance in dealing with their self-conflicts. The HelpCo production line was the scene of a case that illustrates the behavior of upward therapy. The recipient was Joan, a first-line supervisor, whose recent conduct had baffled her subordinates. According to Linda, a production worker, Joan was "losing touch with reality." Joan's conduct was the topic of discussion among line workers for several days both on and off the job. Most claimed she was acting strangely because of a recent divorce, although a few suspected she had more deep-rooted problems. Joan eventually broke her silence and approached Linda and several other workers individually, explaining that she was having domestic troubles and needed people to "help her through this difficult time." Most workers under her supervision were cooperative, and the matter ultimately resolved itself over time.

Although therapy is common in all parts of the postbureaucratic organization, its frequency and intensity vary across the enterprise. Among the professional ranks, where equality, homogeneity, and intimacy are greatest, therapy is most frequent and intense. On the production line and across departments, where inequality and social distance are present in moderate levels, authoritative and partisan social control appears now and then. Downward conflict is sometimes handled through discipline, lateral conflict through vengeance and settlement, and upward conflict through rebellion. Managers, for example, occasionally reprimand and threaten subordinates, restrict their movements, and withhold privileges such as promotions or pay raises. Peers sometimes attack each other verbally, while superiors occasionally resolve lateral disputes by fiat. Subordinates rebel against managers once in a while, mainly by defying their authority. Blackian theory predicts this variation. It also explains why, as we shall see in subsequent chapters, discipline, vengeance, settlement, and rebellion are more commonplace and more potent in work settings with high levels of inequality and social distance such as slave plantations, serf estates, colonial mining camps, and early factories (see Black, 1990:43–49, 56–58, 1993:151–154). In these settings, the moral order is violent rather than therapeutic.

The patterns of social control discovered and described in this book reveal a broader therapeutic trend in modern society. As a number of scholars have observed, people in the contemporary world are increasingly likely to define and respond to deviant behavior as an affliction that requires some form of treatment (Conrad and Schneider, 1980). Those who abuse alcohol, act violently toward their children, or are simply unsatisfied with their lives have access to a growing number of books and services as well as an assortment of specialists willing to provide help (Rieff, 1966: ch. 8). People also have an expanding list of psychiatric categories in which to trace problems with the self (Davis, 1997). Organizations, as dominant institutions in the contemporary world, may therefore be manifesting more widespread changes in human relations. If so, this book has implications beyond the study of one kind of enterprise. By examining social control in the therapeutic corporation, we get a glimpse at one of the emergent moral orders in modern life.

# TWO

# HelpCo

## A Postbureaucratic Organization

L ike people elsewhere, members of organizations frequently define and respond to deviant behavior in
ways not easily detected by outsiders. Studying conflict in the
postbureaucratic organization therefore requires extensive
fieldwork. Conducting research at a single setting can be especially fruitful for obtaining empirical material on social control
as it unfolds during everyday life in a modern corporation.[1]

This chapter describes the corporation featured in upcoming
pages: an employee-owned manufacturing firm. It is a setting
with all the characteristics of a postbureaucratic organization—
equality, homogeneity, and intimacy. I also review is the research methodology, which, following Blackian theory, takes
the conflict "case" as the unit of analysis.

### Inside the Corporation

The organization that is the central focus of this book—given
the pseudonym HelpCo—is a high-technology corporation that
designs, manufactures, and repairs electronic components for

clients in the telecommunications industry. HelpCo is located on the outskirts of a small city in the eastern United States, about 100 miles from a major metropolitan area. A two-lane country highway leads to the plant, where almost 200 employees arrive each morning from their homes in the city and nearby rural areas. From the exterior, HelpCo looks much like any other modern manufacturing firm. Scores of late-model automobiles and trucks line the parking lot. An American flag flies over the large one-story building where employees spend their workdays. The company logo is prominently displayed near the front entrance.

Upon entering the plant, one immediately enters a reception area and sees a banner that reads "HelpCo—An Employee-Owned Company." A number of small plaques, indicating the various awards the firm has received, adorn the walls and are visible as well. On the coffee tables in front of two modest-looking brown leather couches are several notebooks filled with newspaper clippings and copies of magazine articles describing HelpCo and its "progressive" organizational practices. A young woman who sits behind the reception desk cordially greets each visitor.

Shortly down the hallway leading from the front lobby is Pete's office and an adjacent conference room. Pete is the president of HelpCo and like everyone else in the company is referred to by his first name only. He is one of the few people at the plant to regularly wear a necktie. Yet Pete hardly fits the stereotype of a corporate executive. He is a self-described "down-to-earth guy," proud of his sense of humor and gregarious personality. Pete does not spend much time in his office. When not meeting with clients or representing HelpCo at local or national business conferences, he is likely to be mingling with employees elsewhere in the building.

The remainder of the plant is divided into two main sections. On one side of the building is the operations department, where more than 100 workers build and repair small electronic devices that are later shipped to industrial clients throughout the United States. Employees work alongside their immediate supervisors in several large rooms. A few individuals are quiet and keep to themselves. Most, however, carry on with their neighbors or sing along with music on the radio while they work. People are dressed casually; both men and women wear blue jeans and T-shirts. Several times during the day workers can be seen socializing in a large common area that also serves as a lunchroom. Hanging on one lunchroom wall is a sign that announces an upcoming meeting of "The Worker Advisory Committee." Another bulletin lists the names of employees running for election to the corporate board of directors. The latest price of a share of HelpCo stock, written in large numbers on a poster board, is also hard to miss.

On the other side of the plant are the engineering, marketing, and finance departments. To the outsider, the engineering department appears to be in disarray. Schematic drawings and electrical boards are scattered about on people's desks and on the floor. An eclectic group of engineers sits at a large table discussing plans to reconfigure the design of a popular but soon to be outdated HelpCo product. At a small work station nearby, two other engineers are engaged in a heated exchange about an arcane technical matter. The marketing department looks somewhat frenzied as well. Several people are seated at their desks talking on the phone to clients and sales representatives in different parts of the country. Others are meeting in a small conference room debating a new advertising plan. Not far from the marketing department is the more calm and orderly finance department. Working in an environment mostly predictable from one day to the next, employees perform routine accounting and bookkeeping tasks. Like other departments, the work space is open and individuals frequently socialize with each other throughout the day about work-related and other matters, including favorite television programs, romantic involvements, and weekend activities. Most employees in the finance department also have regular contact with individuals in other parts of the company.

The social characteristics of HelpCo employees are immediately evident while touring the plant. The racial distribution mirrors the predominantly white population of the adjacent small city and surrounding area. Except for a black female production worker, all employees are of European ancestry. The distribution of men and women reflects traditional stereotypes. All upper-level managers are men and all secretaries are women. The engineering department is exclusively male, and the marketing and finance departments are evenly split along gender lines. In the operations department, just over one-third of the workforce is female. Most workers, male and female, are young. Whereas the executives are in their forties and fifties, the overwhelming majority of employees are in their twenties and thirties.

## The Formal Organization

HelpCo was founded in the mid-1960s by an engineer previously employed with a large multinational electronics corporation. Initially, the company operated in the founder's basement, where he and a small staff of young engineers operated a consulting business. In the early 1970s, HelpCo expanded its operations to include the development and production of small electronic components. Later in the decade, the company started to focus most of its efforts on the growing market for computerized office equipment. During the 1980s, HelpCo experienced its most successful period, with sales growing at an annual rate of almost 20 percent. By the early 1990s, revenues had reached almost $10 million a year.

The number of people employed at HelpCo has risen steadily over the years, forcing the construction of several additions to the current facility. Growth has also led to a gradual formalization of the company's operation. In the early days, a small team of engineers would not only design and manufacture products, but were responsible for marketing and bookkeeping as well. Today the company is structured much like a traditional corporation, with separate departments for operations, engineering, marketing, and finance. Operations, the largest department, comprises three divisions: production, repair, and shipping. A small human relations department was established in the mid-1980s.

The chain of command has also become more elaborate as the company has grown (see Figure 2-1). At the top of a corporate hierarchy is Pete, the president, who succeeded the founder in this role in 1990. Pete has "risen through the ranks," having been at HelpCo since its inception, where he worked as

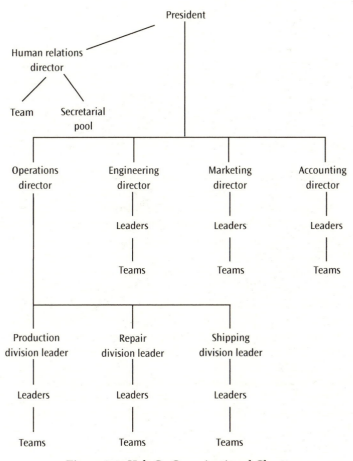

Figure 2-1  HelpCo Organizational Chart

one of the original "basement boys." Reporting directly to Pete
are five *department directors.* Ollie (operations) started on the
production line at HelpCo in the late 1970s and was promoted
to director in 1988. He is known for his serious no-nonsense
demeanor. Ollie describes himself as a "workaholic." Eric (engineering) is a veteran of the computer industry. He joined the
HelpCo executive staff in the early 1980s. Colleagues describe

him as extremely intelligent, but rather disorganized. Mike (marketing) is a recent hire, having been with the company just less than a year. With more than twenty years of experience in the auto industry, Mike embodies the classic salesman. He is energetic and spirited, constantly promoting the merits of HelpCo and its products. Frank (finance), who has been at the firm since the mid-1980s, is described by employees as the most "laid-back" executive. He has an academic background and currently teaches at a local university two nights a week. Before becoming a director in 1988, Hugh (human relations) had been a part-time consultant with the company. He is an Irish immigrant, with an MBA from an Ivy League University. Hugh's office is in a quiet area apart from the hustle and bustle of daily activities. It has the look and feel of a psychiatrist's office. A large couch takes up much of the room, and lining the walls are several bookshelves with selections from Sigmund Freud, Carl Rogers, and other well-known twentieth-century psychologists.

Several middle-level mangers report to the department directors. Below Ollie in the hierarchy are three *division leaders*: Patrick (production), Ralph (repair), and Steve (shipping). These division leaders and the remaining department directors oversee *team leaders*. Each division in the *operations department* has several teams. Those on *production* teams spend most of their work days assembling equipment according to preestablished, though largely informal, guidelines. *Repair* workers diagnose and fix malfunctioning equipment purchased from HelpCo. Workers in the *shipping* division coordinate the flow of products as they enter and leave the plant.

The *engineering department* is composed of several temporary project teams, each responsible for the development of a new project or modification of a present product. At the start of each project, members debate the proper way to proceed. After a general strategy has been devised, tasks related to research and design are assigned to specific individuals. Engineers constantly consult each other during the process and coordinate their activities near the completion of the project.

Three teams comprise the *marketing department*: a small market research group, a somewhat larger sales force, and a team of marketing representatives. Via formal tracking studies and informal interviews with potential clients, members of the research team examine the electronics market for recent trends and possible niches that HelpCo can exploit. Based on ideas generated from these sources, members of the group, along with a team leader who coordinates their activities, periodically present their suggestions to the engineering department. Each sales representative is responsible for marketing the firm's products in a particular geographic region in the United States. Although they rarely see each other, they talk regularly over the phone, comparing experiences, suggesting selling approaches, and determining appropriate strategies for marketing new products. Marketing representatives, who work at the plant, are responsible for taking small orders from one-time buyers and repeat orders from established clients. These employees are on the telephone most of the day.

Employees in the *finance department* work on either an accounting or bookkeeping team. These teams meet formally at least once a week and discuss issues such as reporting procedures, policies for delinquent payments, and new computer software. Finance employees work in a large office separated only by short partitions and thus are easily able to communicate informally. Also part of the finance department is a small team of administrative assistants organized like a secretarial "pool" (see Kanter, 1977:71–73). Instead of being assigned to specific individuals, HelpCo secretaries receive work (mainly letters and other documents to be typed) from employees throughout the company.

The newly formed *human relations department* contains a two-person personnel team and a human relations specialist. The personnel team coordinates hiring decisions and employee benefits, helps produce the company newsletter, and organizes various recreational activities. Hugh, the department director, currently serves as the human relations specialist. Much of his time is spent establishing and running training programs. Hugh also meets with employees to discuss what he calls "people problems." The nature of Hugh's involvement in the social control process, and most importantly his direct and indirect participation in the application of therapy, is addressed in later chapters.

## The Structure of Social Relations

Despite its conventional features, including a well-defined hierarchy and a standard division of labor, HelpCo limits its dependence on bureaucracy. It is a postbureaucratic organization: Social relationships are relatively equal, homogeneous, and intimate.

### Equality

Considerable authority at HelpCo is delegated to employee teams, which are responsible for many decisions affecting daily operation of the firm. Some of these decisions concern issues not directly related to the work process. In the recent past, for example, teams have formulated and implemented policy on smoking privileges, workplace attire, purchase of office equipment, and design of corporate letterhead. Team leaders generally play a limited supervisory role. As managers, they are responsible for making sure team activities run smoothly. Team leaders are also required to evaluate the performance of those under their supervision. Much of the time, however, they participate as relative equals working with fellow team members.

Besides authority over issues directly related to their jobs, employees across the firm have input in corporate-level matters. Unlike traditional capitalist enterprises, HelpCo is owned by the employees rather than outside shareholders. An employee stock ownership plan (ESOP) was established in the late 1970s, which gradually transferred ownership of the company from the founder to employees themselves. It operates like a profit-sharing plan, but employees receive annual contributions of stock rather than a portion of corporate earnings.[2] Along with ownership comes increased input in company affairs.[3] Employee owners vote annually for a nine-member board of directors. The board is responsible for selecting the executive staff (the president and department directors) and approving major corporate decisions. Currently, four members of the board are employed at HelpCo—two department directors, one team leader, and one production worker. Of the remaining five members, two are management consultants working in the community, two are local attorneys, and one is a professor at a nearby university.

As part of their ownership privileges, employees have almost unrestricted access to financial information about the company. In most corporations, financial matters are solely the concern of executives. At HelpCo, information about investments, revenues, and expenditures are available to all employees. The walls of the company lunch rooms are covered with charts and graphs showing monthly sales and profits for different products. Several notebooks containing copies of business plans, new ventures, and systematic comparisons with competitors are also easily accessible, kept in a small room near the front lobby.

Other information on corporate affairs is disseminated to employees by the Employee Ownership Advisory Committee, a group of seven individuals elected by their peers. This committee meets weekly and publishes a quarterly newsletter distributed to employees. The newsletter includes items on employee ownership in general (such as articles on favorable legislation stories about other employee-owned companies) and HelpCo's particular ownership plan (such as the value of shares and the percentage of stock controlled by nonexecutive employees). The committee actively tries to get employee feedback. To this end, they have organized several company-wide meetings to explain features of the plan and have conducted surveys on employee satisfaction with the ownership plan. The committee also acts as a liaison with upper management, meeting with the president and department directors at least once a month. A final responsibility of the committee is coordinating the annual vote for the board of directors.

### Homogeneity

One consequence of a bureaucratic division of labor is the development of distinct subcultures across the organization. Although HelpCo employees occupy specialized positions, several features of the company promote a homogeneous culture. First, the company draws heavily from the local population, with the result that most employees share a white middle-class background. The corporation also attracts individuals with a strong commitment to electronics. As Todd, an engineer, notes (all employees' comments are excerpted from interviews; see the subsequent section "Method: The Conflict Case"): "We tend to be electronics nuts. We always talk about it, always think about it. A lot of us have lots of projects we're working on at home. I think it would be very hard to stand it here if you weren't somewhat obsessed with electronics."

Once hired, employee ownership ties people's fates to one another and gives them a common interest in the well-being of the enterprise. A high degree of internal mobility also breaks down functional barriers. Many employees have worked in more than one department and several have experience in more than two departments. Especially common is movement from operations to engineering and vice versa, although employees have also transferred from engineering to sales and from human relations to operations. This practice, sometimes known as "job rotation," gives individuals a broader perspective of the organization. It reduces the possibility that people will become too provincial, knowing only one part of the company (see Kanter, 1977:271–273; Ouchi, 1981:48–54).

Regular cross-departmental interaction has a comparable homogenizing effect. Frank, the director of finance, describes how this aspect of HelpCo's social environment differs from more bureaucratic settings:

> Here, I know what the guys in engineering or sales are up to. We don't have to worry so much about "suboptimization" so much, where the head of the department just tries to make himself look good, and will do anything to do so even if it means screwing other departments.

Company-sponsored extracurricular activities also enhance a shared corporate culture. These activities include picnics, parties, award ceremonies for employee achievements, and "theme weeks" during which individuals don attire related to topics such as "The 1950s" and "The Wild West."

## Intimacy

The social environment at HelpCo is conducive to the formation of strong interpersonal ties. Individuals form especially close relationships with fellow team members. Many of these friendships extend beyond the workplace. Several directors regularly play squash together, and a group of employees in operations golf on the weekends. Romantic relationships also develop with some regularity. At the time of this study, at least six employees (three couples) were "dating," and at least two employees were involved in an extramarital relationship with each another.

Employees also have many opportunities to develop close ties with those from outside their departments. Several organizational-level committees promote interdepartmental intimacy. One such committee is the previously mentioned Employee Ownership Advisory Board. Another is the fifteen-member New Market Task Force. Meeting every other week, its main responsibility is exploring potential markets for HelpCo's products. Another active interdepartmental committee is the newsletter editorial board. This six-member committee edits a quarterly newsletter that describes various aspects of life at HelpCo, including new hires, employee biographies, company-sponsored events, and examples of work-related humor. Finally, some committees come together for temporary matters. In the past, small groups of employees have organized the annual company picnic, the Christmas party, and "Employee Ownership Week."

Informal exchange across departments occurs with some regularity as well. Engineers, for example, work with marketing researchers and production team leaders when determining the feasibility of new products. Likewise, sales representatives and division leaders in operations regularly discuss the timing of product shipments to and from the plant. The frequency of informal, cross-departmental interchange is evident in the constant movement of employees within the firm. When visiting the company, it is common to see several people in the hallway walking to or from a department other than their own. All of this is enhanced by the small size of the plant: Employees can walk from one end of the building to the other in just a few minutes.

### Bureaucratic Variation

Most employees are aware that HelpCo is unique. While many individuals have not worked elsewhere and cannot make comparisons, some have experience in more conventional firms. Eric, the engineering director, describes how life in the large computer firm where he previously worked differed from his present experience:

> We [managers] would refer to the floor where executives were housed as "mahogany row." No one went near the place unless they called you. We all knew our place in the chain of command. It was a very intimidating. To get ahead you had to cover up your mistakes, and smell the winners. Here you don't have to kiss up to anybody. It's a much freer environment. If you are mad about something, you can go straight to the president, who is just down the hall.

Jane, a production worker with one-year tenure, compares HelpCo to her previous employer, an apparel manufacturer:

> At [the apparel firm] you were always on the lookout, and when the "big man" [plant manager] came around, you didn't even smile, you just looked down and acted busy. Here, hell, the managers will help you out if you need it and bullshit with you. They don't look over your back.

Steve, the shipping division leader, also notes significant differences between the work environment at HelpCo and his former employers:

> I worked in the steel industry for a number of years, so I am very well versed in the antagonism that can go on between workers and management. In a union environment it was you versus them [management], and they knew it. Supervisors were outright pricks. They would sneak around trying to catch people doing stuff. It was a no-win situation. You just don't see that here.

Finally, Elaine, an accountant who had previously worked for a large consumer goods manufacturer, has similar impressions: "HelpCo's a lot more open and laid back. My other company was all business. The environment was strictly professional. You were there to work. There was no playing around like we do here."

Although HelpCo as a whole has a postbureaucratic organizational structure, there is some variation across the firm. The most significant difference is between individuals in professional positions and those performing what is typically called blue-collar work in the operations department. For one, operations employees have less autonomy than their professional counterparts in engineering, marketing, and finance. This difference is evident in how much discretion employees have in the design of their workdays. Paid by the hour, operations employees are required to work a nine-hour day (which includes a one-hour lunch break). Some work a "flex-time" schedule (any nine-hour period between 7:00 A.M. and 7:00 P.M.), but most are required to be at the plant from 8:00 A.M. to 5:00 P.M. By contrast, professionals are paid a salary and although most work during normal business hours, they come and go as they wish. Engineers sometimes work throughout the night. Reflecting these differences, workers in the operations department are sometimes subject to surveillance. Thus, unlike managers in the engineering, marketing, and finance departments, team leaders in operations occasionally take note of employees who arrive late, take long lunch breaks, or engage in excessive socializing on the shop floor.

The intensity of social ties also varies across the organization. This variation is partly related to differences in turnover. Though lower than industry average, turnover is most common among operations employees. During the nine months of the present study, three production workers voluntarily resigned. One professional, an accountant, announced her intentions to quit the final week of the research. A few sales representatives and engineers have been with the firm more than ten years, but even more recently hired professionals note how easily and quickly they formed close ties with colleagues, who often have shared interests that extend beyond the job. As a result, although many close friendships develop among operations workers, ties are particularly strong among professionals. David, a sales representative, claimed that he and his coworkers are like "brothers and sisters." He explains: "I know this might sound corny, but most of us [sales representatives] are in our thirties and single, so in some sense we are like a substitute family." Similarly, Todd noted that he and fellow engineer Lyle are such good friends that they are able to discuss sensitive matters that they cannot share with their wives.

These patterns indicate that relations are most "postbureaucratic" among professionals. Later chapters show that social control varies accordingly: Therapy is most active at the higher ranks.

## Method: The Conflict Case

Material on social control at HelpCo was gathered following the "trouble case" approach common in anthropological research on law and dispute settlement (Llewellyn and Hoebel, 1941:29; see also Nader and Todd, 1978) and recently applied to several modern settings (e.g., Baumgartner, 1988, 1992; Morrill, 1989, 1992, 1995). This method entails conducting extensive fieldwork with the purpose of collecting cases of conflict. A *case* is any instance in which a party defines the conduct of another as deviant and responds in some way. The response may include private displays of dissatisfaction or public attempts to address offensive behavior. By gathering conflict cases and noting their social structures, it is possible to discover the patterns of social control that characterize any social setting and apply Blackian theory to explain them.

Following this general research strategy, fieldwork at HelpCo was conducted during a nine-month period during 1990–1991. The bulk of the data was collected through interviews with sixty-one employees.[4] Most of these were conducted at the corporation itself, in individual offices and conference rooms. Other interviews were conducted more informally during lunch breaks away from the plant.[5] Several of those participating in the formal interviews were given outlines of an interview guide beforehand.[6] Consequently, a few had prepared for the interview and referred to notes when addressing questions. Three employees (an executive, a team leader, and an hourly worker) proved to be particularly valuable informants.

An important concern in research of this kind is the quality of responses. One might suspect, for example, that employees would be less than honest when reporting their experiences with interpersonal and intrapersonal conflict. Perhaps management-level employees might be preoccupied with showing the company in the most favorable light, or lower-level workers might be reluctant to voice their opinions out of fear of reprisal from superiors. Such concerns were unwarranted. Employees did not hesitate to express themselves, although this often meant making critical comments about coworkers or the company itself.[7] The interviews incidentally revealed the general prevalence of therapy at HelpCo. Several individuals made explicit references to what they believed to be the therapeutic effect of the research on themselves and others.

Though the interviews provided the most useful empirical material, information on conflict and social control came from several other sources as well. I attended meetings with the executives (president and department directors), the human relations department, and the Employee Ownership Advisory Committee. I also had the opportunity to observe employees in their offices and work areas, the lunch room, the front lobby, and at company-wide functions. Written material generated by the company provided additional sources of information. This included in-house employee surveys, company manuals, personality tests, internal newsletters, and press releases.

From these various sources, about 250 conflict cases were documented. The quality of information varied considerably. In a few instances, it was extensive, derived from observation, interviews with the participants, and written documents. For most cases, however, details came solely from people's recollections of past experiences. The main drawback of gathering of empirical material through "memory cases" is the tendency of subjects to highlight their more dramatic experiences of conflict (see Koch, 1974:23–34; Baumgartner, 1988:19). Nevertheless, this approach is necessary in settings where witnessing social control is difficult. Moreover, through in-depth questioning, I was able to obtain considerable material on the more subtle ways in which employees define and respond to deviant behavior.

Besides cases, I recorded general observations about conflict made by HelpCo employees. Included were comments by team leaders on typical strategies for handling deviant subordinates and statements by employees on their usual methods for dealing with troublesome peers and superiors. These generalizations—more than a hundred were documented—were as valuable as the cases. While the cases provide useful descriptions of how employees interpret and react to offensive conduct, the generalizations allowed me to assess the relative frequency of the different forms of social control.[8]

The findings of the HelpCo research are featured in forthcoming chapters. Empirical material on conflict in other work settings, both similar to and different from the postbureaucratic organization, is introduced as well. Chapter 3 examines how managers define and respond to deviant behavior by subordinates. The handling of conflict among peers is addressed in chapter 4, and chapter 5 explores social control directed at superiors. Chapter 6 considers the implications of this research on the future of therapy and social control in organizations and elsewhere.

# THREE

# Therapeutic Management

Social control in organizations is most forceful when it flows down the hierarchy. Subordinates who act out of line may be yelled at, demoted, fined, terminated, and even (in organizations of the past) beaten by their superiors. In the therapeutic corporation, however, managers act more like psychiatrists than disciplinarians. Deviant behavior is considered a consequence of intrapersonal conflict, and social control accordingly attempts to heal the self. Subordinates are often encouraged to seek help for their troubles and frequently discuss them at length with superiors. Managers also attempt to address problems by modifying people's surroundings. This can involve moving someone to another part of the enterprise or changing the organization itself.

### Downward Conflict

Downward conflict occurs anytime a subordinate engages in conduct that a superior defines as deviant. Blackian theory predicts that the handling of downward conflict depends largely on the vertical, cultural, and relational distance between the two parties. The greater the distance, the greater the likelihood and strength of *discipline*, an authoritative unilateral mode of downward social control (Black, 1990:47–49). Like authoritative social control by third parties, discipline is characterized by formalism, decisiveness, coerciveness, and punitiveness (Black, 1993:150). According to Blackian theory, distant inferiors should be subject to explicit standards of conduct and punished by uncompromising superiors (Black, 1993:149–153).[1] As vertical, cultural, and relational distance between superiors and subordinates shrinks, downward social control is predicted to become less authoritative. Therapy should be especially common when social space is small (Black, 1995:836; see also Horwitz, 1990:81–83, 93 n. 3).

Below we see that discipline is in fact strongest in work settings with high levels of inequality and social distance.[2] And it weakens when superiors and subordinates get closer. Discipline disappears at minimal distances, where misbehaving subordinates are treated as victims who are experiencing conflict with themselves and in need of help. Therapy is therefore active at HelpCo, although weak discipline is found on occasion at the lower ranks, where inequality and social distance are somewhat greater than elsewhere in the organization.

## Strong Discipline

The largest gaps—vertical, cultural, and relational—between superiors and subordinates are found in workplaces of the past. Discipline is accordingly more frequent and potent in settings such as colonial work camps, serf estates, and early industrial organizations. Violent punishment is especially common.

Inequality and social distance are well developed in colonial settings, and it is here we find some of the strongest discipline. In southern Rhodesia (now Zimbabwe) earlier this century, for example, white mine owners and their agents imposed violent sanctions on mostly black miners (van Oselen, 1976:128–157). Compound "police," dressed in uniforms and armed with *sjamboks* (leather whips), were responsible for monitoring mine workers and enforcing order. Whipping was a standard form of punishment:

> [A]t the Gaika mine in 1930, workers who missed the first call in the compound at the start of the morning shift, those who fell asleep on the job or left work early, were all given six lashes with the *sjambok*. In 1916 at the King's Asbestos mine, failure to meet the piece-work target on any three days in the month earned twenty-five lashes. (van Oselen, 1976:145)

Even seemingly trivial offenses were punished. Workers who failed to remove their hats while in the presence of mine managers, for example, were whipped for failing to show proper respect. This kind of discipline often inflicted great pain: "Many of the whippings were so brutal that they required more than one man to administer them: the worker was held down at wrists and ankles by the compound "police" while the lashes were administered by the compound manager" (van Oselen, 1976:144).

The serf estate represents another setting with a high degree of inequality and social distance, and a corresponding violent disciplinary system. In imperial Russia, serfs who plowed fields improperly, performed work irresponsibly, acted lazy, or failed to complete work on schedule were subject to various punishments by bailiffs acting on behalf of land owners. Whipping with a *rozga* (a birch rod) was the most frequent kind of discipline:

> Mass floggings in the field were not unusual. One day in May 1829 one elder, seven drivers, and seventy field peasants were whipped for poor plowing of fields. The next month fifty-three serfs were beaten for tilling the buckwheat fields improperly. . . . The following May, sixty-eight peasants were flogged at various times during the month for negligently preparing spring fields. One day in June, a year later, one driver and forty field serfs felt the lash for carelessly plowing a fallow field. . . . And in one rather unusual instance, a driver and twenty-five peasants were flogged when they failed to show up in the fields to

offer a special prayer for rain. (Hoch, 1986:175–176; partially quoted in Black, 1993:152)

In southeastern Italy at the beginning of the twentieth century, boys as young as eight years old would often leave home and school for weeks to work as farm laborers for half the pay of adult men. Punishment was especially violent for these young workers, who were at the bottom of the hierarchy and the most remote socially:

> The boys were sworn at throughout the day. They were beaten or threatened with cudgels, and unfortunate lads were made to run the gauntlet between lines of foremen who lashed their backs with belts. The latter technique was known at the "blood line." More ingenious overseers devised special systems of public humiliation and intimidation, such as making a careless boy who had missed weeds pull out the offending plants with a string tied to one end to the stalks and the other to his penis while the work gangs looked at the spectacle. (Snowden, 1986:30–31)

Relations in early industrial organizations were also characterized by considerable vertical, cultural, and relational distance. Although violence was occasionally used to keep workers in line, owners and their representatives more often relied on fines to punish those who violated company policy. In turn-of-the-century precommunist Russia, where factories were "built like walled fortresses, guarded by watchmen and surrounded by gates" (Glickman, 1984:6–7), workers were fined for various offenses, including tardiness, "disobedience, insolence, bad language, immoral behavior, and bad character" (Glickman, 1984:7). A nineteenth-century British company had explicit financial penalties for workers not abiding by the 6:00 A.M. to 6:00 P.M. work schedule:

> Any workman who failed to keep up with the times was subject to a fine of a shilling; if he earned twelve shillings or more a week the penalty was increased to half-a-crown. Those who lingered unduly over their meals had to forfeit

a quarter of a day's wage. (Ashton, 1955:212, quoted in
Gersuny, 1973:18)

At another English work site, fines ranged from one to six shil-
lings for offenses such arriving late to work, working while
dirty, and whistling on the job (Hammond and Hammond,
1968:17–18; cited in Gersuny, 1973:19).

American factories in the early 1900s had rigid management
hierarchies and a workforce comprised largely of recent European immigrants. These conditions, too, were ripe for strong
discipline. Foremen in many larger corporations routinely fired
workers and blacklisted them so they could not be employed
in the industry or region (Edwards, 1979:53). The Ford Motor
Company had one of the more extensive and punitive programs
of managerial discipline. A "Sociology Department" was responsible for investigating the home lives of Ford employees
and punishing those who engaged in what the corporation defined as improper behavior: "A household dirty, frowzy and
comfortless; an unwholesome diet; a destruction of family privacy by borders; [and] excessive expenditures on foreign
relatives—these were among the reasons for condemnation"
(Nevins, 1954:556; quoted in Gersuny, 1973:28). Condemnation
meant a decrease of 45 percent in the $5 a day wage until the
offender "recanted." Those who did not recant during a six-
month probationary period were fired. The "Service Department," which replaced the Sociology Department in the 1930s,
continued the strong disciplinary system at Ford. A network of
spies and a private police force, which included exconvicts
known for their brutality, were hired to monitor and punish
employees who behaved improperly at work and elsewhere
(Gersuny, 1973:28–29). Termination was a frequent sanction at
Ford, especially for those suspected of engaging in union activities. Members of the private police force also beat workers on
occasion.

As Blackian theory suggests, discipline, even in the most
stratified settings, declines when social distance between supervisor and subordinate is reduced. Thus, foremen in the early
American auto industry were more lenient toward those of similar ethnic background (Gartman, 1986:183). In smaller factories, employer-employee relations were sometimes quite inti-

mate, and punishment was muted as a result. Discipline intensified, however, as companies grew in size and supervisory relationships became more distant:

> At first, foremen, like the entrepreneurs before them, relied on a lax and personal style of supervision, based upon personal friendship rather than upon close, coercive control of workers. But the benevolence of the foreman's reign began to decline rapidly in the years around 1910 in the larger shops, and a harsh system of petty despotism arose to take its place. (Gartman, 1986:183)

The decrease in strong discipline later in the century can be explained by corresponding decreases in both inequality and social distance. Inequality declined as wages increased and employees acquired rights of various sorts from employers and the state. Social distance diminished as employees became culturally assimilated and companies embraced organizational practices that required more cooperation between managers and workers (see Edwards, 1979). Consequently, violent punishment is now rare, largely reserved for migrant workers who labor under conditions somewhat similar to those of early capitalism.

## Weak Discipline

Discipline takes on milder forms when superiors are closer—vertically, culturally, and relationally—to subordinates. Thus, in the contemporary bureaucratic organization, where inequality and social distance are less extreme than in earlier work settings, subordinates are rarely beaten or fined. Instead, they are subject to less severe sanctions such as verbal reprimands, warnings, and restrictions of privileges. Among executives in bureaucratically structured corporations, for example, discipline is frequent but weak (Morrill, 1989; 1995:ch. 3–4). At the headquarters of a large American bank:

> Verbal or written authoritative commands are the most common type of conflict management action by superi-

ors against superiors. They typically consist of directives to subordinates to alter some aspect of their behavior immediately and without question. (Morrill, 1995: 107)

Bank executives may be punished in less obvious ways as well. Those judged to be incompetent may be reassigned to positions of less authority, or they may have their resources "liquidated": "Within this strategy, an executive's unit gradually receives staff reductions, budget cutbacks, and decision making limitations that finally make much of what the unit does perfunctory to the overall operations of the firm" (Morrill, 1995:114).

Although generally uncommon in the postbureaucratic organization, weak discipline is occasionally initiated by managers in HelpCo's operations department, where a bureaucratic structure, including moderate levels of inequality and social distance, is present to some degree. Threats, for example, are sometimes issued to production, repair, and shipping workers. In one case, Joe, a team leader, gave an ultimatum to Marvin, a production worker who periodically failed to show up for work: "One more unexcused absence and we are going to have to seriously consider your future with the company." Gary, a shipping employee who used a company credit card to purchase $100 worth of services at a massage parlor, was issued a different kind of threat. After initially denying the charge when confronted by his supervisor with a copy of the receipt, Gary later admitted his indiscretion and apologized. When he was not forthcoming with a financial reimbursement, his supervisor, Bobby, threatened to tell Gary's wife about his exploits. Gary explained that he would bring in a check the following day, which he did.

Threats are also targeted at groups of HelpCo workers. Marcy, a production team leader, issued one at a weekly team meeting: "A couple of you have been slack about cleaning up at night. Sometimes it looks like a pigpen in here. I don't like to do this, but I'm going to start cracking down. Those of you who have been screwing around better shape up." Despite some initial resentment at being reprimanded, most of those on the team "got the message" and modified their behavior.

The repair division was the scene of another collective threat. The incident followed a discovery by Donny, a team leader, that Mark had been taking long breaks during the late morning to buy food and cigarettes at a local convenience store without making up the time (by either arriving earlier in the morning or staying later in the evening). Instead of confronting Mark directly, Donny called a team meeting and told members: "If you have to leave the work area for some reason during the day, make up the time. It's only fair to others. Please don't make me take further action." At the end of the meeting, Mark requested a private meeting with Donny, where Donny broke down crying and confessed: "I'm sorry, I don't know why I started doing it [leaving and not making up the time], but I've been doing it a couple of times a week, and I won't do it again."

Weak discipline at HelpCo may involve more than threats. Managers can, for example, take away privileges. Daryl had his freedom restricted by Paul, his team leader, for taking lunch breaks longer than his coworkers in the repair division. After several offenses, Paul met with Daryl and told him that in the future he must notify someone on the team before and after taking a lunch break. Subtle forms of deprivation are more frequent. For instance, employees who show continued subpar performance often find themselves receiving smaller than average wage or salary increases. They are also likely to be overlooked for promotions.

Discipline takes on a legalistic character when it applies prescribed standards to deviant conduct. At HelpCo, a "code of conduct" included in the company handbook lists several forms of misbehavior that can be subject to formal punishment (see Figure 3-1). A first offense for rules 1–10 leads to a written warning, the second infraction leads to probation, and the third dismissal. Violation of rule 11 means probation for the first offense and dismissal for the second, whereas breaking rules 12–14 calls for dismissal on the first offense. Formal sanctions can also be issued as part of the normal evaluation process. Employees who show continuing "below average performance" can receive a written warning for an initial evaluation of this sort, probation for a second one, and dismissal for a third.

1. Damaging equipment due to carelessness
2. Contributing to unsanitary conditions
3. Wasting time or loitering
4. Excessive trips to the restroom, extending rest periods, quitting ahead of time
5. Being absent without authorization
6. Threatening, intimidating, coercing, or interfering with fellow employees
7. Soliciting or collecting contributions
8. Making false, vicious, or malicious statements about an employee, the company, or its products
9. Leaving the plant during working time without authorization
10. Dishonesty or lying
11. Reporting to work under the influence of alcohol
12. Falsifying company records
13. Theft of company, client, or employee property
14. Drinking alcoholic beverages or taking drugs on the premises

Figure 3–1  HelpCo Code of Conduct: Prohibited Behavior

While managers have the authority to punish employees for violating the code of conduct, they infrequently do so. Many actions were recorded that appear to violate the rules laid out in the company handbook, but only seven (during 1990–1991) resulted in the application of formal sanctions. All of the recipients were operations workers. Written warnings were issued in four of these cases. Elaine, a shipping worker, received such a warning after several unexplained absences. Another written warning was given to Nick in production, who twice performed a task that damaged an important piece of manufacturing equipment. The other warnings were given to production workers, Bruce and Linda, who repeatedly failed to meet the performance expectations of their team members and leaders.

Also noteworthy are two cases where individuals were threatened with written warnings.[3] Both occurred in the operations department. In the first case, Don was reprimanded for persistent tardiness. Greg, a production team leader, told Don one morning: "It's not fair to everyone else if you are not here. I'm tired of telling you [to show up on time]. If you don't like it, look at what the manual [handbook] says." Tardiness was the offense in the second case as well. Roger, a repair worker, continually worked five to seven hours less than the forty hours a week requirement. After four months of this activity, his team leader Paul advised him, "From now on, I'm cracking down. Start getting your hours right or I'm going to take formal action."

Probation, a second type of formal sanction, is more severe than a written warning. It contains both a threat of future punishment and a restriction of privileges. When HelpCo employees are placed on probation, they are one step away from being fired. In addition, their accrued benefits, including vacation time and stock ownership are suspended for what is normally a three-month probationary period. During the present study, only two employees, both in the shipping division, were subject to this sanction. Andy was placed on probation for purchasing automobile parts (for his own car) on a company credit card. Susan received probation for "chronic" poor performance.

Termination, the harshest formal sanction at HelpCo, is especially rare. When such action is taken, it is usually done in strict accordance with the written procedures. Thus, most employees who have been fired were first given written warnings and placed on probation. In the past, supervisors gathered evidence and built "cases" against deviant subordinates.[4] Only one employee was terminated during the course of the present study. Jill, a bookkeeper, allegedly created an environment that was offensive for her coworkers. When she first started at the company, some of her fellow employees laughed at her "sailor's tongue" and her abrasive treatment of others. However, Jill's team leader Peggy and several others were offended and claimed this kind of conduct interfered with their work. Peggy attempted to talk with Jill and explain why people were upset with her behavior. These conversations made matters worse, and eventually it came to the point where she "literally had no friends at the company." Jill was eventually given a written warning and put on probation before being dismissed less than two years after starting with the company.

HelpCo employees were fired for other matters in the past. Several cases are part of company folklore. One well-known case involved a woman in production who had taken toilet paper from one of the company bathrooms (apparently for use at

home) over a period of several months before being apprehended. Many employees were also aware of a case in which
two engineers were fired for "fudging" the test results of an
important new product. Other examples include a production
employee who was caught drinking alcohol in the lunch room
and a marketing representative who stole a client list, presum-
ably intending to sell it to another firm.

Formal discipline, like all discipline at HelpCo, is largely
confined to the operations department, with its moderate levels
of inequality and social distance. Higher-ranking professionals
in other departments, where vertical, cultural, and relational
gaps are the smallest, are virtually immune to the formal code
of conduct. As Neil, a senior engineer, argued: "They [formal
disciplinary measures] are basically used to beat up guys on the
[production] line when they get out of hand. But for us, the rules
are meaningless." Jay, another engineer, noted that he and his
coworkers regularly violated some of the rules without being
punished. Referring to the policy against making negative statements about the firm, Jay claimed: "Hell, if we didn't constantly
criticize the company we wouldn't be good engineers." Kenny,
a marketing research team leader, voiced a similar opinion:

> I ignore the employee manual because it tends to be ge-
> neric. It treats all people the same. [The formal discipli-
> nary measures] seem to fit the operations guys more than
> the sales staff or other professionals. Many of the rules are
> about when people come and go. Well, many of us work
> odd hours and basically come and go as we please. So the
> rules just don't apply.

Most professionals, in fact, claimed they were unaware or had
only vague knowledge of the formal disciplinary measures.

A similar pattern is found in other contemporary organizations: Those at the bottom of hierarchies are subject to more
discipline than those at the top (Grabosky, 1984:174–175). In
American retail stores, lower-status employees apprehended
for workplace theft are terminated at greater rates than their
higher-ranking counterparts in sales or management positions
(Robin, 1967:603). Likewise, corporate executives with little
formal authority and respect from others are more apt than

those held in higher esteem to be subject to sanctions of various kinds, including verbal and written directives, demotions, and firings (Morrill, 1995:ch.4). Legalistic social control also flows mainly downward at Polaroid, a large manufacturer of cameras and other photographic equipment, where a "strong emphasis is placed on rules (especially absence and tardiness rules) for hourly workers, but up the ranks of the salaries, rules have less import" (Edwards, 1979:151).

As Blackian theory suggests, those at the bottom may escape the rules, and discipline more generally, if they are socially close to their superiors. Thus, Barbara, a shipping team leader at HelpCo, claims she is more tolerant of the misdeeds of an employee with whom she had developed a strong outside friendship. Brian, a repair team leader, made a similar observation. Also significant is the fact that team leaders who impose formal disciplinary measures usually have their superiors "do the dirty work." Removed from the everyday life of work teams, higher-level managers have less difficulty punishing first-line employees with whom they have little relationship.

Formal discipline is suppressed in other hierarchical enterprises where people are heavily involved in one another's lives. Physicians in group practices, for instance, find it hard to sanction fellow doctors. A primary practitioner employed in a small hospital describes his reluctance to punish junior colleagues who violate medical regulations: "I prefer that the administration take disciplinary action . . . because we are all very friendly with each other and it's very tough to work with people and discipline them at the same time" (Friedson, 1975:214). The lenient treatment of police misconduct can also be understood as a product of the low degree of social distance between investigators, who are usually officers themselves, and those being investigated.

Long-term employees are more likely to have close ties with superiors and are consequently subject to less discipline of any kind. In fact, tenure limits one's culpability to a certain extent. Consider the case of Stu, a repair worker who has been at HelpCo for almost twenty years. Several individuals noted that Stu takes extended lunch breaks and socializes excessively on the shop floor. Yet Stu's behavior is generally ignored by Frank, his team leader. Only occasionally does Frank make gentle suggestions to Stu that he be more careful in his conduct. Frank and others claimed that newer employees are not treated so leniently. This pattern is present elsewhere. At a contemporary American automobile manufacturing plant, for example, "high seniority is considered a mitigating factor, so that an employee of long standing may escape punishment for an infraction that would subject a newer employee to a formal penalty" (Gersuny, 1973:53).

## Therapy from Above

Although discipline disappears when inequality and social distance shrink, social control does not. But rather than being punished, subordinates are likely to receive therapy. This form of social control is a regular feature of communes, Japanese corporations, and other settings where people are equal, homogeneous, and intimate. It is also quite active at HelpCo.

Therapy involves several strategies when initiated by superiors. First, managers attempt to *understand differences* among individuals and what are regarded as their distinctive personalities and backgrounds. Superiors *let people help themselves* as much as possible, and often encourage them to *talk through problems*. Therapy from above may also include efforts to *change the environment*, the assumption being that self-conflicts are influenced by people's larger surroundings.

### Understanding Differences

The first stage of therapy usually involves the exploration of circumstances thought to be causing personal difficulties. During this diagnostic phase, blame and condemnation are discouraged in favor of toleration and acceptance. Members of the Bruderhof, an American spiritual commune founded in the early twentieth century, "will often try to ignore deviance if it is not deemed a threat to the system" (Zablocki, 1971:230). The Bruderhof brotherhood attempt to understand people's "unique personalities" through observation and discussion (Zablocki, 1971:224–225). A similar orientation toward deviance is found among the Amish of North America, who are well known for their cooperative living and working arrangements: "No matter how serious the offense, the Amish never look upon someone . . . as an enemy but as someone who has erred" (Kephart, 1976: 27). They often simply pray and wait patiently for offenders to rectify their mistakes. And in modern Japanese corporations, where employees work in family-like social environments, "it is often necessary to live with internal problems for a long time" (Rohlen, 1974:113). Termination is a rare occurrence, reserved for grave or criminal offenses: "Incompetency . . . is no excuse for firing someone" (Rohlen, 1974:79–80).

Managers at HelpCo respond similarly to troublesome behavior. First, attempts are made to understand the source of alleged difficulties. Problems are frequently linked to matters unrelated to the workplace. One HelpCo supervisor, for example, understood the slipping performance of a female production worker as a consequence of "going through a painful separation with her husband." Another employee in the production division was determined by his team leader to be suffering from "an emotional collapse" after his only daughter moved to a nearby state to marry a young man known for his "wild ways." The employee's week long "slump" was interpreted as a response to this tumultuous event.

Managers may seek the assistance of others when trying to understand the nature of employee self-conflicts. In a common scenario, a supervisor approaches a peer or superior who is familiar with the troubled individual, and together the parties try to discover underlying factors that may be responsible. Family life, financial matters, and overall mental and physical health are likely to be considered, as are "pressures" directly related to the work environment such as the offender's relationships with other employees.

Hugh, the director of human relations, often intervenes to help managers diagnose subordinates. When his assistance is solicited, Hugh generally follows a process of getting supervisors to "verbalize the problem." In one case, Hugh met with Donny, a team leader, to discuss the subpar performance of Timothy, a well-respected junior employee in the repair division. Donny was bothered by a sudden drop in the quality of

Timothy's work. Hugh encouraged Donny to describe what was happening in Timothy's life at the time. As their conversation proceeded, several issues were "brought into the open." For one, Timothy had recently moved into a new home, an event that allegedly added stress to his life. Moreover, a bright and energetic new employee had been hired in Timothy's work group. This move apparently threatened Timothy's position as the most knowledgable repair person. Hugh and Donny determined it would be best to see whether Timothy's attitude improved as he became more comfortable with his new living arrangement and new coworker. According to Donny, time healed the problem. Timothy was "back to normal" about a month later. Walter, a marketing team leader, requested Hugh's assistance when he encountered problems with Nick, a recently hired salesperson. Through feedback from other employees and several customers, Walter discovered that Nick had a "personality that did not fit this company or the industry." Nick evidently alienated others by acting as a "know-it-all." After reflecting on the matter and citing similar behavior observed in others, Hugh and Walt determined that Nick was "covering up his lack of functionality [knowledge about the business] with his [aggressive] personality." They concluded that Nick's limited experience in the industry would hinder any attempts to help him deal with the problem. Hugh and Walter decided it was best to contemplate the matter before approaching Nick. Shortly after their discussion, however, Nick resigned because, according to Walter: "He evidently realized that he didn't have a whole lot of friends here, nor did he have friends in the industry, and thus decided he didn't have a home here."

Hugh sees his role as helping supervisors uncover the hidden sources of employee self-conflicts as an important one. He does not, however, always agree with the diagnoses offered by supervisors who seek his assistance. On some occasions, Hugh criticizes managers for failing to understand employee personalities. In one case, for instance, Hugh suggested to a production team leader that his concern over an employee who was a "loner" may be unwarranted. Hugh claims: "Some individuals are different, and have their own reasons for acting the way they do, and people [supervisors] have to realize that. This person [the 'loner'] is a good worker. He just isn't as outgoing as the rest of the group."

The strong emphasis on understanding differences means that behavior considered as unsatisfactory may be tolerated for some time. Thus, a production team leader waited six months before saying anything to two employees who constantly arrived late for work. In the finance department, an accountant's constant "bitching" was ignored for several weeks by his supervisor. A young engineer's tendency to arrive at work smelling of alcohol was endured for almost a month. And a secretary who continues to act unprofessionally in the presence of clients, by joking with coworkers and making personal phone calls, has never been told to modify her conduct.

Managers generally have a limit on how long they will refrain from taking action. Still, they may endure problems for a considerable length of time. Theresa, a team leader in finance, described an employee in her work group who had been with HelpCo for three years as having a bad attitude and below-average performance record. The troubled employee, Kelly, has never been confronted: "He just does his own thing. I'm sure if we had to let somebody go, he would be the first, but he somehow gets along." Similarly, a production team leader's abrasive behavior toward others (he frequently yelled at coworkers) was tolerated for over a year even though his supervisor was quite bothered. When refusing to take immediate action, supervisors typically hold the therapeutic view that the offending party is suffering from a temporary problem that will heal itself over time.

Management's unwillingness to condemn subordinates is not necessarily appreciated by everyone. Several individuals, in fact, commented that they wished their supervisors were more aggressive in dealing with those who misbehave. Along these lines, Cindy, a production worker, noted: "There is a saying that 'once you get hired here, you have a job for life.' Unfortunately, that is true. We put up with some pretty poor performances for a long period of time." As Danny, a production worker, agrees: "You have to try awfully hard to get fired from here." The comments of Ralph, the repair division leader, reflect a general reluctance managers have about dismissing employees:

I've been involved in several instances [where someone was fired] a while back, but I didn't like it. It's especially hard if we have to let them go for performance reasons, as opposed to not fitting in, because it usually means they are a good person, they really tried. I hope it never gets easy, though. If it does, then something is wrong with me.

## Letting People Help Themselves

While patience is considered a virtue, it has its limits. Conflicts with the self are not tolerated forever in the therapeutic corporation and similarly structured settings. Even so, superiors rarely demand change. Instead, subordinates are encouraged to help themselves. Supervisors often approach others and make subtle allusions to their alleged problems. The hope is that troubled individuals will engage in self-reflection and realize that some kind of change may be in order.

This practice was common in the Oneida religious community of nineteenth-century New England, where members shared community property and successfully operated a furniture-manufacturing enterprise. Individuals who violated informal standards of conduct would voluntarily come forward and acknowledge their infractions before a group of well-respected members (Kephart, 1976:68–72). At the Bruderhof commune, most deviance is also reported by offenders themselves: "The Bruderhof socialization process is designed to make it a torment to withhold information about oneself on any matter" (Zablocki, 1971:225). As a result, members regularly seek out others and make "unsolicited confessions." The Bruderhof are compelled to confess even their innermost negative thoughts, including sexual fantasies expressed in dreams (Zablocki, 1971:193). On Israeli kibbutzim, collective agricultural enterprises where material goods are shared among members, various mechanisms are used to persuade offenders to admit their misdeeds and seek help. Traditional holiday celebrations, where the entire community is present, provide an opportunity to make not so subtle references to individuals who may have acted out of line. An observer, who lived on a kibbutz in the 1950s, described a case incorporated in a skit associated with the Jewish festival of *Purim*:

In the *Purim* skit, there was a pointedly witty scene de-
voted to the unnamed, but easily identifiable, young men
who refused to accept an assignment in the dairy. . . . The
reaction to the "dairy" skit was immediate. The following
day when [I] was working in the fields with one of the
young men, the latter spontaneously referred to the skit
and voluntarily admitted that he had been seriously af-
fected by it. (Spiro, 1956:100)

The offenders were reportedly more cooperative in the future
when asked to take on unpleasant work assignments.

Similar practices occur at HelpCo, where employees are persuaded in various ways to help themselves. Consider how Dean,
a production team leader, responds to workers who appear to
be experiencing difficulties:

I usually try to deal with it first on the [shop] floor. I might
approach the person and talk about a football game or
something, and then say, "How are things going?" I let
them take the initiative, to admit that something is bothering them that might be affecting their work.

Charlie, another team leader, prefers a more direct approach.
But he, too, is gentle:

Sometimes I have to sit down with them and say, "What's
going on?" And they will often respond, "There's nothing
bothering me." Then I say, "Come on, something is bothering you, what is it?" And if they still don't want to talk
about it, I'll tell them, "Okay, but if you want to talk with
me at some point, I'm all ears." You see, I have to be
careful not to hurt anybody's feelings.

Hank, an engineering team leader, makes an explicit therapeutic reference when describing the nature of his intervention: "I
kind of take on the role of psychologist. I don't tell them what
to do because they know the answer. If you help people solve
their problems the first time, you are less likely to have to do it
again." Managers hope by simply bringing up troublesome matters, subordinates will "get the message" and take remedial action.

Many employees believe they have an obligation to help themselves. Jay, an engineer who had fallen behind in his contribution to an important project, traced the source of his trouble to a tendency to get too involved in coworkers' activities:

> Part of my problem is that I love solving other people's problems. A lot of time I help people when I really shouldn't. I've made commitments of my own and don't really have the time. But I feel like I can't help it, that's just the way I am. Just recently we got a new piece of computer software and I spent two hours a day for a week teaching two guys how to use it, and of course my work got put aside. I talked to my supervisor about it, but ultimately it is my responsibility.

Although some self-conflicts are handled without the assistance of others, people at HelpCo may, on their own initiative, seek help from managers. This behavior is akin to voluntarily seeing a psychiatrist. In one instance, Randy, a production worker, sought assistance for his "motivation" problems. He remembered his first few weeks on the job: "I didn't really like coming to work. And when I got here, I was lazy and really didn't do the kind of job I was capable of [doing]." After several months of frustration, Randy approached his supervisor Greg and explained his dilemma. Greg, previously unaware of Randy's difficulties, offered some advice. As Randy explained:

> He [Greg] told me that he had been there too [in the same position] when first with the company. He was young, didn't really have any responsibilities, and didn't like the idea of getting up and coming to work each day. But he changed after he got to know people here and realized that a job like this one is not easy to come by.

Though Randy did not change immediately, he is now seen by several managers as an "ideal employee" and is currently being considered for a team-leader position. Randy reflected on his past: "My attitude has really changed since back then. Getting married and having a kid has also made a difference."

Similarly, Kyle, a team leader in accounting, commented that several members of his team have solicited his help over the years:

> I've had a number of people [on my team] come to me when they've had outside problems and tell me things like, "I've been making a lot of mistakes the last couple of days and I'm not talking to people because of what's going on in my life." It's not as if they are making excuses. Sometimes I don't even know their performance is hurting. And whatever the issue is, it usually gets better when they come talk to me, although I may say very little.

### Talking through Problems

Individuals in the therapeutic corporation do not always confess their sins and heal themselves. Managers sometimes take a more active role in the therapeutic process by having individuals talk through their problems. It is assumed that simply talking and "getting things out in the open" can be helpful. Here, social control most resembles modern psychotherapy.

Talking through problems is a customary practice in communal settings everywhere. In the Oneida community, "criticism" was a popular form of therapy: "One version of criticism [was] called historical criticism . . . which, to the modern mind, has a surprising flavor of Freud and more recent psychiatric thinking" (Robertson, 1970:131). Individuals subject to this kind of social control met with a committee of esteemed members, who encouraged the discussion of problems that, according to the founder of the Oneida community, "in the past had been laid secret, perhaps half forgotten, but are necessarily darkening and poisonous to present experience." (Robertson, 1970:131). Senior members of the Bruderhof commune, "who are skilled diagnosticians of attitudinal failings" (Zablocki, 1971:226), counsel individuals on a regular basis. Counseling is geared toward identifying the "deeper disturbances" said to be causing members to think and act in inappropriate ways. Deviant conduct is defined as something individuals have little control over but that can be cured by having people discover the sources of their internal problems and talk about them.

Counseling sessions are also common throughout HelpCo.[5] This practice often begins with a manager pulling an employee aside, usually in a private office, and discussing the perceived problem at length. Consider first the case of Chuck, a repair worker, who was counseled for a general "attitude problem." According to Debbie, his team leader, Chuck "bad-mouthed virtually every decision that was made in this company." He also attracted "poor performers, who would cry on his shoulders, and he would make them feel better by telling them the company was unfair and that everyone had it out for them." Ollie, the director of operations, eventually became aware of Chuck's disruptive conduct and pressured Debbie to take some action. Debbie recounted what happened:

> Ollie and I met with Chuck first and told him what we thought was going on. I think we lowered his self-esteem to almost nothing. He evidently didn't know how we felt about him. Then just he and I talked. We discussed how he carries everyone else's problems around with him, which makes him feel important and some of the other workers feel good, but in the long run brings him down and hurts him. We met again a week later and he said he couldn't push away those people [who like to cry on his shoulder]. So he asked if he could be transferred to another group, which I arranged. Now he is doing better though I still think he likes getting attention in unhealthy ways, like stirring up trouble for the sake of it.

Individuals may also receive counseling in response to specific events thought to be part of deeper disturbances. This was the case when Doug, a team leader in the marketing department, met privately with Rich, a sales representative, to discuss an incident that had occurred the previous day. It turned out that Rich had neglected to inform several clients about the cancellation of a meeting designed to introduce a new product. Angry for having wasted time on an unnecessary trip to the plant, one of the clients contacted Doug and vented his frustration. In response, Doug arranged a lunch-time meeting with Rich. During the meeting, Rich claimed he had been working fourteen-hour days trying to put together a new sales plan and had simply forgotten to contact the clients. Doug also discovered after further discussion that Rich was close to having a "nervous breakdown." To resolve this issue, both parties agreed it would be best if another employee assisted Rich for a couple weeks while he completed the sales plan. Rich's problems apparently remained after he finished the plan. According to Doug, Rich still "has some issues to work out."

In a rather similar case, Eric, the director of engineering, counseled Victor, a young employee who raised his voice at a client over the telephone. Victor was called to Eric's office shortly following the incident and explained that the client had falsely accused the company of shipping a product that did not meet the specifications both parties had agreed upon earlier. Eric responded by noting that "clients are often wrong, but we have to live with them." After some discussion, Victor agreed with Eric's suggestion that in the future sales representatives rather than engineers should handle "difficult" clients. Eric interpreted this incident therapeutically, noting that "they [sales representatives] tend to have the kind of personalities that can deal with angry customers. Sales reps are more 'people persons' while we [engineers] are better with ideas."

Managers vary in how much they listen as opposed to talk when counseling employees. Even when they do all the talking, supervisors refrain from criticizing subordinates or demanding a change in behavior. Consider the case of Danny, a production worker, who received counseling for continually "getting on the nerves" of others. Charlie, his supervisor, understood Danny's self-conflict as follows:

> He was one of those people who tried to be everybody's friend. He tried so hard he would fabricate stories. Someone would say I went fishing this weekend and caught five big bass, he would say he went fishing and caught ten. After a while I knew he was lying, but he was trying so hard to be accepted. I sat down with him and (this was kind of an emotional thing) I told him, "You've got to understand that if someone is going to be your friend, then they'll be your friend, but you can't make people be a friend. You can't buy a friend or lie about yourself to be

accepted." He understood where I was coming from and although it took some time he's better now.

Supervisors sometimes bring in others, usually higher-ranking managers, to help counsel deviant subordinates. Female supervisors are especially likely to do so.[6] When this happens, counseling becomes somewhat authoritative. Blackian theory predicts this pattern: Managers brought in to help are typically more superior and distant than immediate supervisors. In one such case, Debbie, a production team leader, sought assistance one morning when a male subordinate wore a T-shirt with a message that she considered offensive. The message read "Mr. Condom" and depicted a cartoon figure resembling a prophylactic. Patrick, Debbie's supervisor, was made aware of the matter and met privately with Jack, the offender, during a morning break. Patrick suggested that the T-shirt was amusing, but that it may offend some people, particularly those who are religious. Jack reluctantly agreed not to wear the shirt again, though he did make a point of saying he will continue to wear his "Budweiser" T-shirt. Patrick and Debbie understood Jack's behavior therapeutically: They concluded that he "just needs attention" and that insulting people is his way of getting it.

Marcy, another production team leader, sought Patrick's help one morning when several employees on her team were acting boisterous and disturbing other workers. After unsuccessfully persuading the workers to calm down, Marcy approached Patrick in his office and asked for help. Patrick then confronted the group of misbehaving employees, one of whom argued: "Hey, we were just letting off a little steam." Patrick responded in a therapeutic but forceful manner: "Okay, but let's give Marcy a little breathing room. She's been busy and has got a lot of things on her mind so she may get a little upset when she feels like your behavior is partly her responsibility. So why don't we try to show a little compassion." Patrick notes, however, that he does not always side with Marcy: "There are a lot of times where I have to explain to Marcy, who is relatively new, that some of the employees on his team will act differently on occasion. I will tell her to try to get to know their individual personalities."

Hugh, the director of human relations, also helps counsel individuals. His intervention typically occurs after a supervisor suggests to a subordinate that he or she see Hugh in his private office. When treating individuals, Hugh often employs a modern psychotherapeutic technique known as "transactional analysis."[7] This technique, which was most popular in the United States during the 1970s, is consensual, ultimately relying on offenders to discover their own problems and solutions. As Hugh states: "Once they verbalize the problem they are more than halfway home in terms of addressing what's bothering them." In one illustrative case, Hugh counseled Matt, an accountant, whose supervisor Kyle claimed was "moody": "You never knew from day-to-day whether he would be cooperative or nasty. Sometimes he would just give everybody the silent treatment. It drove me and everybody else crazy trying to figure out when he would be OK to talk to." Frustrated with his failed attempts to get Matt to talk about what was bothering him, Kyle sought Hugh's assistance. After initially rejecting the idea, Matt met with Hugh for about an hour one day late in the afternoon. Matt "opened up" and confessed that he was very insecure in his job. He felt like others knew more than he did and thus he "sometimes got stressed out to the point where he didn't want to deal with anybody." Matt claimed he "felt better" simply by expressing his "feelings." Hugh, who has periodically checked on Matt since the meeting, claims he is "slowly improving his interpersonal skills."

Shortly after his first meeting with Matt, Hugh counseled Ed, who had experienced trouble communicating with his coworkers in the repair department. Again, the hope was that a solution would emerge if the parties could talk through the problem. Yet in this case the troubled employee was prone to silence. As Ed's supervisor Brian explained:

> I couldn't figure out what was wrong with this guy. I would have to talk with him every day about something, anything to make him feel he was important. If I didn't, he would start stacking bricks up, start building this wall. So [then] I have to go talk to him and knock it down. But one time I neglected him for a while and the wall got so

high he wouldn't even acknowledge me. He was completely turned off.

At this point Brian solicited the assistance of Hugh, who met
briefly with Ed during lunchtime. Ed was not especially receptive, although he did agree to end his silence with his supervisor. According to Brian, Ed's future at HelpCo is in doubt: "I
still have to be careful with him. It's funny, he's a good technician, he's smart, but his personality may end up ruining his
career with us."

If Hugh is unsuccessful addressing employee troubles, he
may recommend professional counseling services. Consider the
case of Peggy, an accounting team leader. Shortly after her promotion to team leader, she allegedly started acting "bossy" and
alienating her coworkers. Peggy sought assistance from Hugh.
During their first meeting she broke into tears, claiming that
domestic troubles were negatively influencing her demeanor on
the job.[8] After several meetings, Hugh suggested a local psychiatrist, with whom Peggy has since met several times. She
now "feels better" and refers to time before she sought help as
"back when I was acting all funny." Carl, a marketing employee, was referred to professional help after being demoted
from a management position and becoming, in his words, "extremely depressed." First, he met five times, for over an hour
each meeting, with Hugh. After these counseling sessions, Hugh
concluded that Carl's troubles were deeper and referred him to
a psychologist. Although the demotion occurred four years before this study, Carl says he is still getting over the effects of the
event, which he says was a "personally devastating experience
to go through." Nonetheless, Carl claims that because of professional help and "a lot of soul searching" he has experienced
an "important psychological change" that allows him to function without many "leftover negative feelings." On another occasion, Hugh advised Beth, whose marital problems were determined to be affecting her work in the marketing department,
to attend a local support group where people with similar difficulties meet weekly to console each other. Richard, an accountant with an admitted drinking problem, was directed to
Alcoholics Anonymous. While these cases are consistent with

the general therapeutic nature of social control at HelpCo, they are uncommon. Most therapy occurs in the organization itself.

Unlike a growing number of larger companies in America, HelpCo has not established an employee assistance program, or EAP, as it is commonly called. EAPs are typically administered by human relations personnel, who distribute information and offer counseling services to employees thought to be experiencing "substance abuse" problems related to alcohol and illegal drugs (Trice and Sonnenstuhl, 1990). The assumption is that alcoholism and drug abuse are diseases, and that those afflicted are helped somewhat when they talk to others about their condition.

### Changing the Environment

Sometimes talk is not enough. Managers in the therapeutic corporation may determine that modifying the surroundings is the best remedy for self-conflicts. One strategy transfers an individual to another part of the organization. An underlying assumption is that people will change for the better if they move to settings more suited to their personalities. Among the Bruderhof, this therapeutic strategy is known as a "change of scenery." Offenders are transferred to jobs on other parts of the commune: "A 'change of scenery' is often quite disruptive to the routine of daily life. The Bruderhof doesn't mind this. The exigencies of work must always give way to the 'inner needs' of the community members" (Zablocki, 1971:198).

In Japanese firms, poor performers are sometimes reassigned to positions similar in name but with less responsibility: "People judged incompetent or undesirable are shuffled about in the system without being dismissed or demoted" (Rohlen, 1974: 148–149). When this is done, every effort is made to preserve people's "dignity and status" by giving them job titles that imply importance.

Similar practices are found at HelpCo. Dean, a production team leader, reports how individuals are relocated within the firm:

> If someone is not working out in a particular section of
> the company, we give them four or five different chances

in different positions in order to help them out. Some have been passed around for a couple of years before finding a home. I've had some people come to my section [production] from engineering, where they didn't really fit in, and blossom. Others feel production is too much like a factory atmosphere, and [thus] move to engineering or sales, where they've done great.

Ted, an engineering team leader, makes a similar point:

There are times when people just couldn't get into our job [engineering] because it is so varied, and the atmosphere just isn't right for them. Yet they might do wonderfully in manufacturing. That's happened three or four times, where individuals who seem like really good people are transferred to manufacturing, and they just take off. We had one lady who had a lot of prior training but she just couldn't cut it in this department. She went to [the operations department] and in that environment she rewrote the books on several important procedures. She took a process that had fourteen or fifteen steps and cut it down to five. On the other hand, there are people in manufacturing who hate the repetition and come to work for us and love it. Even if they don't have the technical skills, if they are good people, we'll fit them in, and most of the time it works out.

Phil has done especially well after being transferred. He was encouraged to move from the marketing to operations department after several months of unsuccessful sales work. According to Debbie, a production team leader, Phil is "not a people person, but because he knows a whole lot about the industry, he has been a valuable asset to us."

Although there were no demotions at HelpCo during the present study, individuals have been removed from positions of authority in the past. Marty was demoted from his job as a marketing team leader and returned to the "field" as a sales representative. According his coworker Rich, Marty had poor management skills:

He was a great salesman, but when put in charge of others, he didn't know what to do. He tried to run the show, thinking everyone should act like he did in the field. But salesmen are a unique bunch. We have our own ideas about what works. He didn't realize this. John [the previous marketing director] tried to let Marty know he was in trouble, but he wouldn't listen.

After six months as team leader, Marty reluctantly accepted John's suggestion that he assume his old sales position.

Jim, a team leader in repair, was also demoted for an inability to manage others. According to Ollie, the director of operations:

Jim was the best technician in the company, but he turned out to be the worst supervisor. He couldn't train people and he couldn't lead people. Everybody in his group knew it immediately when he was promoted. We gave him a few months. He just wasn't a good manager. We tried to get him to acknowledge this, but he just didn't see it. We finally had to tell him that he would have to go back to the bench. Unfortunately, he felt like he was being dumped on. He had a big chip on his shoulder. We tried to tell him we wanted him to stay and we liked him, but he couldn't handle it.

Demotion is ostensibly punitive, yet it can proceed in therapeutic terms. For example, Hugh, in his capacity as human relations director, participated in both demotions described above to "provide support." He interpreted this type of action therapeutically:

Just because these people can't handle management positions doesn't mean they are bad people or incompetent. Some people aren't made to be leaders and we shouldn't make them be someone they are not. Now it's not easy being told you aren't a good manager, so we have to be careful not to hurt people in the process and ruin their careers. I'm not always successful, but I try to help.

Even termination, which is punitive since people lose their job and income, can have a therapeutic component. At HelpCo, for example, those responsible for firing people often assume they are helping individuals in some way. Hugh, who meets with every departing employee, notes:

> We usually do what we can to salvage the individual before dismissal. But we shouldn't think that we here at HelpCo have some magic potion that makes people stay with us forever. Our environment is unique, and some people just are not going to work out. But if I look back, I can say with some pride that many people who didn't work out have gone to [companies] where they could grow. And I know this because I have helped people find jobs who have been dismissed. I have even kept in touch with a couple of folks [departed employees].

Another way to modify the environment and in turn help address self-conflicts is through group or organizational level change. This response is likely if several individuals are seen as negatively influenced by the work setting. In one notable case at HelpCo, Frank, the newly appointed director of finance, encountered what he defined as a "lack of commitment" by a small team of bookkeepers under his direction: "They were doing their jobs, but they were not as committed as they could have been. They would never volunteer to help others or stay a little later at night if someone needed their help. And they always complained about coming to our weekly [department] meetings." Frank considered these actions as a lingering response to the "authoritarian tendencies" of his predecessor, who, compared with other managers at the firm, ran a "tight ship." Frank's first step was to meet with the bookkeepers and get their ideas. After the meeting, he decided to make two group-level changes with the hope of improving attitudes and "helping people grow." Most significantly, Frank greatly reduced his authority over the group. Bookkeepers were given responsibility for matters previously controlled by the director, including the assignment of specific work tasks and the purchase of office equipment. In addition, their system of pay was changed from hourly wage to salary. According to Frank, the bookkeepers' morale improved considerably in the six months after the changes were implemented. He did note, however, that one woman remained "committed to the old way of thinking."

The operations department was the location of another group-level change. Here, again, the change was therapeutic, designed to help people overcome intrapersonal problems. Paul, a repair team leader, instituted such a change after becoming concerned with what he viewed was a "downhill shift in the way people in [my] group were getting along." Several times he had witnessed employees bickering and refusing to cooperate with one another. In response, Paul conducted a written survey of the group's attitudes about the team. As he explained:

> Two or three people wrote lengthy answers saying they felt ignored. They wanted me to be more involved in the group. I was shocked because I thought they didn't want a strong leader. But I guess they felt they wanted someone to guide the group, and to be there when they needed someone to talk to. Because my team has grown a lot in the last few years and is one the biggest in the company, I couldn't possibly take care of all their needs. So I met with my supervisor and we decided to split the team in two, which meant adding another team leader. This has seemed to work all right. Not all the problems are gone, but people are much more cooperative.

At various times throughout HelpCo's history, managers have made organizational changes that do not seem directly tied to particular acts or individuals. Although not obvious, such changes—which included the reduction in the layers of management, the formation of a company-wide task force, and the introduction of employee ownership—may be classified as therapeutic. They are attempts to modify employee psychologies by changing the social environment.

Blackian theory predicts that discipline will be common and strong in organizations where superiors and subordinates are separated by great distances in vertical, cultural, and relational space. And reality conforms to the theory. When inequality and social distance are extreme, workers are subject to violence and other punitive forms of social control. In the therapeutic corporation, where social space is small, therapy replaces discipline. The self becomes the focus of downward social control. Psychologies are examined, individuals help themselves and talk through their problems, and surroundings are modified. Managers consequently take on a new role. Rather than being disciplinarians, making sure people obey rules, they act more like psychiatrists, helping individuals overcome their alleged problems.

# FOUR

# Therapeutic Peacemaking

Not all organizational conflict is downward. People also define and respond to deviant behavior by their peers. Though peers have no formal authority over each other, they regularly engage in social control. Peers may pursue conflict through physical and verbal attacks, for example, or managers may intervene and pacify disputes by separating and scolding the adversaries. In the postbureaucratic organization, where hierarchy is weak and peers are socially close, lateral conflict is handled less aggressively and authoritatively than elsewhere. Combining elements of therapy and conciliation, social control helps individuals address their intrapersonal problems and restore harmony to their damaged relationships. Most conflict is handled by peers themselves, although managers sometimes lend assistance as mediators.

## Lateral Conflict

Lateral conflict occurs when a party defines the behavior of a peer as deviant or otherwise undesirable. Like downward conflict, the amount of social distance between parties is important in predicting how lateral conflict is handled (Black, 1990:44–47, 53–58, 1993:154). Black theorizes that the most severe *vengeance*—aggression between equals—occurs when adversaries are separated by large distances in cultural and relational space (1989:44–47).[1] Vengeance is often violent and frequently reciprocal (Black, 1993:150).[2] It is less formal than discipline, which punishes offenders for violating rules. When equals punish each other, as happens with vengeance, they tend to be capricious, touchy, and concerned with honor (Black, 1993:154).[3] Also significant are the presence and location of higher-ranking third parties who may intervene as settlement agents (Black and Baumgartner, 1983:113; Black, 1984:24, 1990:56–58, 1995:836). If third parties are present and are elevated above and socially distant from equal adversaries, conflict may ultimately be handled through nonpartisan *settlement* (Black, 1990:56–58). As noted earlier, Blackian theory predicts that settlement becomes more authoritative as vertical, cultural, and relational distance between third parties and adversaries increase (Black and Baumgartner, 1983:113; Black, 1984:24, 1990:56–58, 1995:836).[4] Recall, too, that the authoritativeness of settlement also varies directly with the social distance between the adversaries themselves (Black, 1995:835). Thus, when equals are homogenous and intimate, and the distance between them and their superiors is small, both vengeance and settlement should be uncommon. According to Blackian theory, lateral conflict is, instead, handled by the adversaries themselves in a peaceful manner with an emphasis on informality, compromise, voluntariness, and helpfulness (Black, 1995:836). Superiors may become involved, but their participation is generally limited to a mediator role. Rather than impose an outcome or even evaluate the merits of cases, mediators simply help parties resolve their own differences (Black and Baumgartner, 1983:100–102).

Baumgartner's (1992) research on disputing among children draws on Blackian theory, and her conclusions are particularly relevant for understanding lateral conflict in organizations. Because children are under almost constant supervision of adults, they have few ties to each other and rarely develop the means to address their differences amicably. Most conflict between children subsequently gets handled in one of two ways: aggression or authoritative intervention by adults—or in other words, via vengeance or settlement. Thus, childlike behavior, such as pushing, shoving, and whining to get the attention of adults, is the result of the subordinate position of children rather than their age (Baumgartner, 1992:17–31). This general pattern, where mutual inferiority promotes hostility between parties and the likelihood their disputes will be settled by superiors, extends to the workplace. In many organizations, workers are in the same structural position as children, and their conflicts are handled similarly. The first sections of this chapter present material showing that vengeance and settlement are in fact most likely when conflict occurs between workers under a strong hierarchy. As Blackian theory predicts, therapy and conciliation emerge in settings like HelpCo, where managerial authority over employees and social distance among them are minimal.

## Vengeance

The handling of lateral conflict in organizations with strong authority structures often includes mild forms of vengeance, including behavior that might be considered childlike. Consider assembly line workers at a large manufacturing plant in the northeastern United States (Balzer, 1976:40–41). Foremen closely monitor their activities and, like school children, they respond to a bell that rings at the beginning and end of each shift. Workers handle conflict among themselves by yelling, teasing, crying, and engaging in petty violence. Several cases illustrate the patterns of lateral social control found in this workplace. One case involved a woman who recently transferred from the evening to the day shift, where she had to learn new skills. After making several mistakes, a coworker yelled at the woman for allegedly making the entire work group look bad. The woman said nothing, but started to cry. Another coworker confronted her and took her to the bathroom to calm down. When she wiped away her tears, the aggrieved woman vowed: "I'll get her back, just you watch. I'll get even with her." In another case at the plant, a young male worker accidentally knocked into a female colleague, causing her to lose concentration: "She started screaming at him. As he walked away she hit him. He swung and threatened her saying, 'Don't you ever do that again because the next time you do, I'll put you through the wall.' Nothing further happened but neither talked to each other for a long time after that" (Balzer, 1976:41). Another worker was ostracized for being "physically and socially awkward." He was the butt of many jokes and whenever he entered the company dining area, other workers, acting much like children in a school lunchroom, would either ignore him or end their conversations and stare at him (Balzer, 1976:41).

Dock workers on the American West Coast labor under similar conditions of subordination, and they, too, respond to misbehaving peers in aggressive and "childish" ways. The most serious infraction is to "slack off," so that other members of the crew are overworked:

> The foremost offense that one longshoreman can deliver to another is to shirk his share of work so that more work is shifted onto other members of the work crew. Various techniques are used, from offering to fight to simply sitting down and making the offender do all the work for a time. (Pilcher, 1972:99)

Embarrassment and ridicule are also used to punish coworkers. So is violence. The aggressive nature of conflict in this work setting is evident in a case described by an anthropologist who studied a longshore community for several years. Dock workers all have nicknames, many of which contain profane words and phrases. An informal code dictates that they should not be used outside of the work context. It is generally not a serious offense to violate this code:

> In the presence of women, however, the use of a nickname usually produces a violent retort, and in the presence of the man's family may be productive of violence. In one instance, a man's nickname was used in the presence of his wife by one of his best friends to which he replied by battering the offender into insensibility, and this extremely violent response was not felt to be excessive by either the other longshoremen or the victim of the attack. (Pilcher, 1972:105)

Peers at HelpCo attack each other less frequently and aggressively than dock workers. Verbal attacks are the most frequent way of exacting revenge, although violence is not unknown. Consistent with Blackian theory, vengeance is mostly confined to lower-ranking workers in the operations department, where hierarchy is somewhat greater than elsewhere in the firm. Two HelpCo production workers, for example, were observed engaging in several "shouting matches." According to a coworker, they "just rub each other the wrong way and yell at one another about virtually everything." Vengeance takes other forms as well. A woman in the repair division, for example, directed a derogatory hand gesture ("flipped the bird") at a female coworker after the two argued about a mutual boyfriend. And Cindy, a production worker known for her bad temper, received a series of short unsigned notes from Bert, a fellow employee, that suggested she transfer to another department. These incidents were reported to Joe, her team leader, who decided to investigate the matter. No one was willing to take responsibility, although several employees knew the perpetrator. Bert quit the company after only several months on the job. Only then did Joe discover that Bert was the culprit.

Only one violent confrontation between peers was documented at HelpCo. It was a mild incident: Two women in the production division exchanged a few slaps. The conflict started when Beatrice made comments about Rose's husband and his alleged infidelities. The scuffle ended several seconds after it began when a fellow worker convinced them to stop. Two cases, both in the operations department, were recorded in which individuals threatened others with violence. In the first case, Ricky was upset with Jack, a production coworker, for mocking his especially strong southern accent. After voicing his displeasure, Ricky threatened to attack Jack with a knife. Following the incident, Charles, their team leader, met with Ricky and suggested that his behavior was inappropriate. Interestingly, the aggressor's behavior was defined somewhat sympathetically by Charles: "He is from the backwoods, and that's how they settle things there." Several women in the operations department were the recipients of a second threat of violence. Alice, a shipping clerk, issued the threat—"I'll beat the shit out of you"—when a coworker stared at her boyfriend one day when he came to take her to lunch. Now when Alice's boyfriend visits the plant, everyone on her work team turn their head or walk away.

Although vengeance is less common among those at the higher ranks, it may appear if the social conditions are right, mainly if the adversaries are socially distant. In bureaucratic organizations, for example, interdepartmental conflict—where parties are differentiated by function, physically segregated, and versed in specialized corporate languages—is handled more aggressively than intradepartmental conflict (Morrill, 1992:71). Although HelpCo employees from separate departments work closely with each other and share a corporate culture, they are more distant than individuals belonging to the same department. This distance creates conditions under which interdepartmental conflict occasionally takes on a contentious character. For example, several disputes between engineering employees and marketing staff were characterized by loud verbal exchanges, insults, and other aggressive measures such as "memo wars" and the building of coalitions to intimidate opponents. One interdepartmental verbal battle made its way into HelpCo company folklore. This dispute was part of ongoing conflict between Eric, the director of engineering, and Steve, the shipping division leader. Most of their disagreements were about the proper way to develop product prototypes. According to several employees familiar with the case, both had strong and uncompromising personalities, and as a result, their disagreements often erupted into loud quarrels. During one particularly heated debate Steve called Eric a "motherfucker." Barry, a shipping division team leader, chose a less confrontational mode of vengeance. Over the course of several months, he wrote nasty memos to express his frustrations with team leaders in marketing and engineering. Recipients of these memos learned to ignore or ridicule what they sarcastically called "BarryGrams."

Because the most severe vengeance is associated with social distance, such behavior can only be expected when the adversaries are kept apart by physical space or some other obstacle to intimacy. At HelpCo, few such obstacles exist. Even so, peers may deliberately avoid each other, thus allowing hostilities to continue. For example, in one longstanding conflict, Patrick, the production division leader, and Walter, a marketing team leader, chose to correspond only in writing (through "memos") after many heated arguments about product development. Walter wanted the production division to play a limited role in the development of new product lines, whereas Patrick believed he and others in his division should have more input in the process. This dispute continues; both parties do their best to avoid each other. When required to be in each other's presence, they do nothing more than exchange pleasantries. Longtime adversaries Ted and Bob also avoid each other and keep distance between themselves. Bob, a senior marketing research employee, refuses to attend meetings where Ted, an engineering team leader, is present:

> This man [Ted] is impossible to deal with. He is so arrogant. He thinks he knows everything. Now, we all like to think our way is the best and that we are always right, but you have to compromise, and he won't. I don't think he means to do it, but his attitude turns people off who have to work with him. Most other people have learned how to put up with him, but me, I have less tolerance for his kind of behavior. So when I get around him I just get so angry I can't even talk. My solution was to back off [and] just not deal with him anymore.

Adversaries at HelpCo often find it difficult to stay apart. Hostilities thus quickly subside. Moreover, third parties, who are usually close to both of the adversaries, are likely to defuse rather than escalate conflict. As Blackian theory predicts, socially close third parties ("warm nonpartisans") normally encourage people to work out their differences rather than take sides (Black, 1993:135). So whereas aggressive behavior sometimes leads to lasting animosities, it is most often accompanied by conciliatory gestures. Combatants normally make up. A conflict between Ralph, the repair division leader, and Patrick, the production division leader, is typical. The two were embroiled in a protracted dispute, complete with several shouting matches, over company expenditures. After two weeks of fighting, Ralph decided he had enough. He visited Patrick's office one morning as if nothing had happened. Ralph informed Patrick that he had just closed a deal on a new family home and then invited him to lunch to celebrate.

Timothy, a repair team leader, handles his aggressive encounters in a comparably conciliatory manner: "I get in my share of shouting matches, but I usually feel bad after the fact. I never really apologize, but I go out of my way to be nice to the person [I argued with], and try to get things back to [the way the were] before." Brad, an engineer, also emphasized the importance of maintaining collegial relationships:

> It's hard to stay mad around here very long. You have to see each other all the time. It's a small company so we can't let little squabbles interfere with our daily relationships. So if I do get angry and start yelling, it's only for a day or so. I usually realize how stupid it was to get upset over something so minor.

Vengeance does not persist when social distance is small.

The tendency for lateral aggression to be held in check is also characteristic of other work settings where ties between employees are strong. Thus, in companies where executives are members of small interdepartmental teams, vengeance is common but short lived: "Moreover, the longer executives are involved in disputes with the same colleagues, either as opponents or supporters, the more they come to share the same understandings and language, and the more likely they are to negotiate their differences" (Morrill, 1992:72). Consider, too, small worker collectives. People work closely with each other and relations are frequently tense. According to a member of a collective on the West Coast of the United States: "What happens is that there are really basic personality conflicts. Real differences in character traits. People feel strongly about doing something in a certain way. It's a matter of style" (Jackall, 1984: 118). She describes how disputes among her peers in the collective are settled:

> [D]isputing individuals take different shifts, avoid situations where disputes will erupt and, in general, back off their quarrels, establishing what are basically armed truces with one another. The group facilitates such pat-

terns of accommodation by rearranging schedules and so on, and acts as a silent patrol to enforce the truces (Jackall, 1984:121).

As with HelpCo, the closeness of social space reduces vengeance.

### Settlement

The social conditions that produce vengeance are also favorable to settlement. Thus, in settings with strong hierarchies and peers who are equal but distant, superiors frequently intervene and settle disputes. When hierarchy is extreme, settlement takes on its most authoritative form, "repressive pacification," the goal of which is to end "conflict as quickly as possible, violently if necessary, without regard to the consequences of the parties" (Black and Baumgartner, 1983:106). Repressive pacification is especially common in work settings where colonial supervisors oversee subordinates hired from native populations (see Black and Baumgartner, 1983:106). Early in the twentieth century, for example, black mine workers in southern Africa were punished simply for engaging in conflict. If two workers happened to get into a physical altercation, which they often did, both would be beaten by white supervisors or locked in company jails for several days (van Onselen, 1976:143–145).

Conflict in contemporary bureaucratic organizations is frequently settled by superiors, although less authoritatively than in hierarchical work settings of the past. Among executives at the headquarters of a large American bank:

> [Settlement] most often occurs spontaneously at . . . executive meetings, unsolicited by the disputants. The chair of the meeting, usually a direct superior of those in conflict, intervenes between the disputants with a few words such as "I think this discussion has gone far enough." (Morrill, 1989:398)

Bank executives also pacify disputing subordinates by reassigning them to less important positions so that "in effect, they are jointly punished for their dispute" (Morrill, 1995:129).

Although uncommon overall at HelpCo, settlement is most likely and most authoritative in the somewhat bureaucratic operations department. Ed and Mark, for example, were interrupted one afternoon by Paul, their team leader, while loudly arguing over the proper way to repair a complicated high-selling electronic device. Paul simply told the parties: "Quit wasting your time and get back to work." In a second case, Jenny, a shipping team leader, intervened in a conflict between two female workers who had been disputing for several weeks over a mutual love interest. Frustrated with the behavior of the two, Jenny called both parties aside and gave them an ultimatum: "Get along or be subject to a written warning." Both ignored each other for the rest of the week or so before gradually returning to the congenial relationship they had before the conflict.

Settlement between higher ranking HelpCo employees is rare. As Blackian theory predicts, when settlement does occur, it is usually interdepartmental, where social distance is greatest. However, it is less authoritative than settlement at lower levels of the organization. Higher-ranking managers act more like judges—considering the merits of cases and rendering enforceable decisions—than repressive peacemakers (see Black and Baumgartner, 1983:104–106). Two conflicts were adjudicated at HelpCo during the present study. The first was initiated when Irene, a sales representative, became angry with Andy, a shipping team leader, for neglecting to deliver a new product to several clients on the East Coast. Andy claimed he was never notified about the delivery. Irene, however, suspected that Andy was not cooperating with her request because of his lasting animosity from recently having been passed over for a sales position. Worried that Andy may repeat this failure, Irene notified Mike, her supervisor, who in turn met with Steve, the shipping division leader. The two supervisors listened to both parties before concluding that Andy was at fault. He was not punished but was told he would be reprimanded the next time he ignored a request from the marketing department.

Thomas, a marketing researcher, and Aaron, a senior engineer, were principals in a second adjudicated conflict. This dispute began after Aaron made plans to "push" an expensive new product on the market. Thomas resisted Aaron's efforts, claiming the product was loaded with "bells and whistles" (a term used to describe a product with many decorative but unnecessary accessories) and would not sell because its price would be prohibitive to most potential buyers. After several verbal encounters between Thomas and Aaron, their respective supervisors (Mike and Eric, the marketing and engineering directors) interceded and eventually sided in Aaron's favor. The product was put into production about a year later. As Thomas noted, however, he got the "last laugh" because the product has sold poorly since its introduction.

These cases are anomalies. When superiors become involved in lateral conflict at HelpCo, their intervention is usually non-authoritative. In most cases, however, managers do not involve themselves in the conflicts of those under their supervision.

## Therapy and Conciliation

Conflict is handled more peacefully and cooperatively when peers are under weak authority from above and are socially close to each other and their managers. People frequently just *accept others* for who they are and engage in self-reflection and self-therapy. Even so, peers regularly *express feelings* in order to help each other address what are defined as intrapersonal problems. They may also attempt to reconcile differences and *seek harmony*, with managers acting as mediators. These patterns are prominent at HelpCo and other settings resembling the postbureaucratic organization.

### Accepting Others

HelpCo employees are initially inclined to accommodate the imperfections of peers. The comments of Frank, the director of finance, reflect a widely held belief:

> We all know people here whose personality traits aren't too pleasant. But you learn to live with it. It's like your family. My mother does a lot of things that someone outside my family wouldn't understand. But because she's my mother I accept her the way she is. To a degree you

see that kind of attitude here, where someone will do something that's really rotten, but you will say to yourself "Yeah, he pisses me off, but that's the way he is." You recognize peoples' personalities and their strengths and weakness, and you work with the strengths and try to minimize the weaknesses.

Lisa's remarks about Stephanie, a coworker in the repair division, also illustrate a general belief that one should accept people for who they are and attempt to work around their bothersome tendencies:

I just knew right away we were going to clash. You know some people just aren't made for one another. But there is really nothing you can do. It's not like it's their fault or your fault. You just try to deal with the person, even if every little thing they do drives you nuts.

Voicing similar sentiments, Steve, the shipping division leader, describes how he and his coworkers respond to their frustrations with Jeff, an engineering colleague:

Every so often, Jeff enters into a silent war with everybody. He just clams up, closes his door and doesn't talk to anybody. Then two weeks later it's over. I don't know why he does this. But we've come to the conclusion that he is just not a people person. And when he goes into one of his "moods," we just leave him alone and wait for him to get over it.

Stacy, an accountant, shares the views of others, but is a bit critical of people's reluctance to handle differences openly:

A lot of personality conflicts in our department don't get handled very well. Everybody waits for them to go away. [People] don't always come out and say, "This is what you're doing and it really annoys me." Some of us are very timid, and we just wait to see if what is bothering us will stop. And often [we] just adjust to the person or the situation.

These same tactics are favored by individuals who are part of close-knit egalitarian relationships in more conventional organizations. Physicians in some settings, for example, respond to misconduct in ways similar to HelpCo. An observer noted how conflict was handled among doctors of equal rank in a small group practice:

> In some instances, the offense was normalized as something the offended himself might do "unconsciously" or in a "weak moment" or "on a bad day," and thereby justification for complaining to the offender or about him to others was denied. In other instances, the offense was perceived as an outcome of the biography of the offender— his habits, training, or personality—which, since it could not be changed, provided justification on functional grounds for failing to respond to it by complaint. (Friedson, 1975:216)

This observation is supported by the comments of a primary practitioner describing how he deals with irritating colleagues:

> I came to the conclusion that I'm not going to educate them. This is such a deep-seated personality problem and I would hurt them more than gain by their becoming self-conscious and the anxiety becoming more aggravated. Since there is no evil intent involved, there is nothing I can do to change their personality but to accept the situation as it is. (Friedson, 1975:213)

Consider also school administrators, whose jobs require them to work closely with one another:"[O]rganizational members are likely to identify particular perspectives with the people and groups who espouse them and, when conflict between perspectives occurs, to displace these differences in perspectives onto personality conflicts" (Bartunek and Reid, 1992:118). One particular conflict at a large high school, as described by an ethnographer, was defined and pursued in a manner comparable to several of the cases described above:

> [T]he conflict that assumed central importance during the year for Mary Anne and other school personnel was an

interpersonal private one between Mary Anne and Karen. As one dimension of this conflict, both Mary Anne and Karen made personal attributions about the other. Karen said Mary Anne was personally unsupportive, and Mary Anne came to see Karen as overdependent and, possibly, "the wrong personality" for the academic director position. Other people made personal attributions about Karen as well. For example, the business manager said Karen was more gloomy than she should be and, after the evaluation, Karen and Judy began to describe Karen as personally overconcerned with power. Karen eventually came to view herself as "borderline stupid" and as having made a jerk of herself. (Bartunek and Reid, 1992:136)

Karen's interpretation of her own conduct as part of the problem mirrors a pattern found at HelpCo. In fact, accepting others often means turning to the self and changing one's behavior in some way. When this occurs, the conflict gets transformed into an intrapersonal one. Rather than attempting to help someone else, the individual engages in self-therapy.

Most HelpCo employees engaged in self-therapy at one time or another. A typical case of self-therapy was initiated by Donny shortly after he was promoted to team leader in the repair division. Danny claimed that he became troubled when fellow team leaders neglected to invite him to managerial luncheons. With the help of a pamphlet on interpersonal communication ordered from a management journal, he concluded that his personality was to blame. Donny then began an effort to educate others about his "tendency to turn people off by seeming aloof." He now goes out of his way to explain how people in the past often misinterpreted his shyness for arrogance.

Employees may also engage in self-therapy as a response to specific events. Consider the case of Aaron. He had become upset with Marty, a marketing employee, for delaying a meeting three times between the two to discuss the modification of a small piece of electronic equipment. After the third cancellation, Aaron hung up the phone without responding to Marty. He then left the building and went to a local restaurant. Aaron had lunch and "cooled down" for almost two hours. He returned to work and phoned Marty to reschedule their meeting, which finally occurred a week later. Aaron reflected on this incident:

> I'm the type of person that likes to be on time and to keep commitments once they're made. Other people are not like that, and I've got to realize that. But when it constantly happens, it starts playing with your mind. And [in this one case] I got mad. I lost control.

Todd, a young engineer, behaved in a like manner when team member Brad stated one morning that he had made a change in the design of a new product. Upset that his peer did not consult him, Todd's initial response was to comment sarcastically "Okay, fine" and walk back in anger to his work station. Todd then notified Hank, the team leader, that he was taking the rest of the day off. Describing the situation later, Todd blamed a sleep deficiency for his actions:

> When I came in that day, I didn't feel very good because I didn't sleep that much the night before. When I reacted the way I did I felt terrible, but I knew it was a lack of sleep that caused me to react that way. Rather than just get more upset, it was better for me to leave. When I came back after the weekend [the incident occurred on a Friday], I felt great. I realized it was stupid to get upset over something so minor. So I apologized to him.

Todd concluded that he needed to "work on himself."

Self-therapy can involve changing not only one's personality, but one's appearance. Consider the case of Irene, a marketing representative. She depicts her experience with several uncooperative shipping clerks: "When I would go down to [the shipping work area and] ask for something, they would basically ignore me. It was like pulling teeth. I hated dealing with them." After experiencing this problem for some time, Irene determined that she needed to change her outlook toward others. She concluded that her formal business attire intimidated the clerks and caused them to be troublesome. In response, Irene began dressing more informally:

I've found that they [the shipping clerks] relate to me and everyone else in this department [marketing] if we are dressed like this [in blue jeans]. Before we were walking around in our silk blouses and heels and they [the shipping clerks] were down there with jeans and tennis shoes. And when you wanted something from them they would be thinking, "We know who makes all the money in this company, the sales department. Why should we go out of our way for you." Now we've gotten away from that. We dress more like them and they relate to us a lot better.

When examining and attempting to change themselves, individuals may seek out others for assistance. Employees at HelpCo frequently discuss their intrapersonal problems with coworkers and, in some instances, family and friends. Accordingly, many individuals have confidants, usually someone on their work team, to whom they can turn if they have difficulties. Senior employees are especially likely to take on this role. Among those who discussed their workplace tribulations with family members was Jason, a recently hired accountant. He was "hurt" because his fellow workers did not include him when they socialized at lunch and after work. According to Richard, a coworker, Jason talked about the matter periodically with his wife for several months before eventually leaving the firm. Phil in operations often talks to his wife about how to improve his "self-esteem" at work. Likewise, Beth, a marketing representative, and Neil, an engineer, regularly discuss their work-related "stress" with their spouses.

## Expressing Feelings

While accepting individuals for who they are and turning to the self are common practices, people at HelpCo and in other decentralized communal settings often directly express their feelings as a way to help others and themselves. For example, among the Bruderhof brotherhood, "if a person has a grudge against, or a criticism of, another person, he is required to go directly to that person and speak to him about the problem. Keeping resentments to oneself or gossiping are . . . strictly forbidden." (Zablocki, 1971:195). A member of the Twin Oaks commune voiced similar sentiments: "Gossip in our definition is talk that does damage. Exasperated comments on the quality of someone's work is gossip, as are disparaging remarks about personal characteristics. If you have something negative to say, says our rule, say it to the person's face" (Kincade, 1973:150–151). Even so, though many conflicts at the Twin Oaks commune are handled informally through face-to-face encounters, members of the community worry that self-expression and attempts to help others may be suppressed if parties are forced to confront each other directly. To combat this fear of confrontation, one member has taken on the role of "Generalized Bastard." His main responsibility is to relay information, often unpleasant, from one party to another (Kanter, 1972:27). He usually approaches an individual and mentions the nature of the problem, yet he does not name the party who solicited his help. Sometimes, the Generalized Bastard encourages the parties to discuss their differences in person, holding the therapeutic assumption that many conflicts are due to "overriding personality traits that need to be discussed" (Kincade, 1973: 153). The goal of this practice, according to one member, is to reduce gossip and not make "other people uncomfortable" (Kincade, 1973:153). In the Oneida spiritual community, peers (like subordinates) were often subject to "criticism" for their misdeeds. People were constantly encouraged to verbalize their displeasure with themselves and others. In fact, it was considered harmful not to express one's frustrations. So strong was this belief that community members even criticized those who were no longer living: "Deceased members whose diaries or letters were found to be incriminating might find themselves being subjected *in absentia* to a 'rousing criticism' " (Kephart, 1976:72).

People at HelpCo also put a premium on expressing feelings. The comments of Pete, the company president, reflect a widely held position: "Those who make it here [at HelpCo] are those who handle their problems in an open way, those who aren't afraid to let others know how they feel." Although this advice is not always followed, people regularly share their feelings with peers. These therapeutic encounters usually involve one party attempting to help a coworker in a nonthreatening and occasionally humorous manner. Encounters take on a somewhat more authoritative character, resembling counseling sessions, when the helper is a more senior employee or a group of employees. When the helper is lower in rank, go-betweens are likely to approach those receiving help.

A typical therapeutic encounter begins when one party informally approaches another. Consider a case in which Brenda, an accountant, confronted coworker Dwight and expressed concern that he leaked sensitive corporate information about a new product venture to several people in town. This encounter took place during a company-sponsored volleyball tournament in the early evening. While standing together waiting for their team to play a match, Brenda casually told Dwight that going public with this kind of information can be harmful to the company. Dwight reluctantly agreed that he had made a mistake, but later came to define his conduct in therapeutic terms, as a consequence of a general tendency of wanting "to show off to people by bragging about how much he knows." For her part, Brenda was greatly relieved after the encounter. She was concerned that Dwight might "feel bad." The marketing department was the scene of another therapeutic encounter. One morning, Ann overheard Scott, a newly hired coworker, acting rude to a client over the phone. After the incident, Ann explained to Scott that the best way to deal with difficult clients is to "kill them with kindness." Scott, defining his actions therapeutically, confided to Ann that he sometimes would lose his "cool" in tense situations. He agreed to work on his "problem" in the future.

Individuals may express themselves in brutally honest ways. Frank, the current director of finance, described an especially candid meeting with Earl, a former director of engineering. According to Frank, Earl had an intolerable personality:

> He was so obnoxious. I remember telling him one time, "When it comes right down to it, I really don't like you." There are very few people I would say that to, but this guy was unbelievable. He would attack people when they were down and enjoy it. What he would do was harbor stuff about people and hit them at a low point, after they've made a mistake. This wasn't fair. People couldn't defend themselves. It was done seemingly just to hurt people. It was funny though, because if you were to meet him, he would be thoroughly charming. And most of the

time he was, but when he saw a chance to jump on someone he would. I'm not sure what caused him to do this.
He was brilliant, but really had problems with other people. He finally quit to start his own business. I think it
[working on his own] will better suit his personality.

Once in a while, a small group of individuals will confront
and express their feelings to coworkers thought to be experiencing difficulties. These encounters resemble therapeutic "in-
terventions," where friends of drug-addicts or alcoholics are
ambushed by a group of close friends and forced to address their
"problems." Such encounters are somewhat more authoritative
than one-on-one confrontations. Consider the following case,
initiated by three financial clerks after Anita, a fellow employee, collected money for a home interior party but spent the
money on personal belongings instead. When the group of
women discovered what happened, one of them, Carrie, asked
Anita about the incident after work in the company parking lot.
Anita initially denied the charge but eventually claimed responsibility. The following day Carrie and two coworkers sat
down with Anita and explained to her that they felt "let down."
Carrie believed Anita was having financial problems at home
and that "her behavior was not something she would normally
do." While Anita eventually returned the money, her relationship with others was strained for several months after the affair.

Encounters are also more authoritative when parties expressing themselves are slightly higher in rank than those who are
defined as needing help. Although peers by definition have no
formal authority over each other, they nonetheless may differ
in rank. Some employees, for example, receive higher wages
than others. Thus, salaried professionals have more rank than
hourly paid workers, and employees with long tenure tend to
be higher in rank than recently hired employees. A common
pattern has higher-ranking parties attempting to "educate" their
coworkers. One such case was initiated by Randy, a young production worker, who accused Jay, a senior engineer, of "slack-
ing off" for reading magazines at his desk. While Randy's remark was made in the context of a joke, Jay was nonetheless
concerned that his actions were mistakenly perceived. As a result, Jay explained to Randy that he was reading trade maga-

zines to catch up on the latest developments in the electronics industry. Jay believed he was helping his fellow employee by showing how product innovation benefits the company. Kenny, a marketing employee, sought to educate Ed, a repair worker, in a case similar to the one just described. This case began when Ed approached Kenny in the lunchroom and told him: "You must have such an easy job, coming in to work at noon [every day]." Kenny described his response:

> Often I will ignore these types of remarks, but here I felt I had to explain myself. He saw me come in at noon, but what he didn't see is that I was here 'till midnight last night and that I was at a trade conference over the weekend. I think it is important that we educate these guys [in operations] about what we do so they understand our [marketing] role.

People sometimes invoke humor during attempts to educate their less experienced coworkers. David, a senior sales representative, did so after pulling aside Lyle, a junior engineer, who had verbally expressed his skepticism about a product while meeting with an important client. David explained to Lyle that while his suspicion may be warranted, it is not good business to expose product weaknesses in front of those who purchase them:

> This guy [Lyle] scared me to death [laughing]. He was too honest. I tried nudging him under the table when he starting talking about the problem with [the product] but he just didn't understand the nature of the beast. So I had to talk with him and explain that we need to present a united front when we meet clients. I'm still not sure if he gets it. These engineers are smart guys, but they aren't businessmen. I thought about not having them at our meetings, but we need them there so they can better understand the clients' needs when designing new products.

Secretaries also attempt to educate each other. Sarah, a senior secretary, tried to help Margie, a younger coworker, who often acted "immature" on the job. Margie's loud discussions of a television "soap opera" were especially bothersome. First,

Sarah tried to explain the importance of acting "professional" for the company and for one's own career. When these efforts failed, Sarah tried to get Margie to join a professional secretary's organization, with the hope this would get her more involved in her job. These attempts were also unsuccessful, although Sarah continued to encourage her younger counterpart to join the organization "for her own good."

This form of help—seeking to educate others for alleged deficiencies—is present in other settings where people work closely with one another as peers. A study of social control in health care organizations, for example, found that experienced physicians would engage in "talks" with junior colleagues who "appeared to have sloughed off, overreferred, or managed a patient in such a way as to cause extra trouble for others" (Friedson, 1975:217). Most examples "of such talk in the medical group were described in terms that conveyed a neutral and educational rather than an angry and critical tone" (Friedson, 1975:217). The nature of these discussions, though largely unilateral, is often therapeutic. As a staff member stated, judgement and condemnation are not considered appropriate:

> There shouldn't be any recriminations. . . . It does harm. Whenever a discussion leads—and now I am taking a psychological slant—to attitudes of guilt, then it is no good. I think the discussion of a mistake has to be on the basis of what one has learned [from it]. (quoted in Friedson, 1975:210).[5]

People in postbureaucratic settings may also try to help higher-ranking peers. Rather than express themselves directly, however, lower-ranking parties are likely to have go-betweens, or therapeutic agents, act on their behalf. This pattern is consistent with Blackian theory. The presence of homogeneity and intimacy means that potential third parties are close to both the initiators of social control and its targets. This condition prevents the development of partisanship and the escalation of conflict (Black, 1993:131–135). Moreover, go-betweens at HelpCo are usually higher in rank than those whose cases they pursue and are similar in rank to those being helped. This has the effect of equalizing cases, thereby fostering conditions for dialogue (see Black, 1990:54). Consider the case in which Frank, the director of finance, served as a go-between in a high-profile interdepartmental conflict. The case was initiated when Mike, the recently hired director of marketing, purchased a forty-dollar ashtray for his office. Anita, an accountant, became aware of the purchase and was angered by it. She voiced her concern to several coworkers, including Frank, the director of finance. Acting on Anita's behalf, Frank met with Mike one morning in a conference room to discuss the ashtray incident. During the meeting, Frank explained to his counterpart in sales that HelpCo was different from other companies and that executive-level decisions, even minor ones, are subject to scrutiny. Mike reluctantly agreed to be more careful in the future. He is now "working on ridding [his] old self," although he remains uncomfortable that his actions are so closely monitored by employees in other departments.

### Seeking Harmony

The focus of help in decentralized communal settings frequently extends beyond the self to the broader relationships among individuals. When it does, social control becomes concerned with reconciling interpersonal rather than solely intrapersonal differences. But like the efforts to resolve self-conflicts, people try to restore harmony to their relationships by talking, often with supervisors assisting in the reconciliation process. Among members of a worker-owned grocery collective on the American West Coast, for example, the most common method of resolving conflict is direct discussion between quarreling parties. Mediators frequently play a role as well:

> People simply talk out their tensions with one another, often during the quiet morning or outside of work over coffee or drinks. Sometimes, when antagonisms build to the point that direct discussion is not possible, other collective members intervene. They talk privately to the individuals involved, try to divert the conflict, defuse it, or make it humorous. (Jackall, 1984:120–121)

A member of the Twin Oaks commune describes how disputes are settled: "When two people cannot get along with each other at all but are nevertheless forced by circumstances to be in each other's company, we sometimes get them together with a moderator and ask them to talk the problem out" (Kincade, 1973: 158–59). Disputes are occasionally brought before the public and the community as a whole moderates conflict.

Many conflicts at HelpCo, including self-conflicts, end when people communicate their feelings to others. And most employees at HelpCo believe it is best to handle lateral conflict without interference from managers. This view is reflected in the comments of Donny, a repair team leader: "When any guys on my team get into a disagreement over how to fix a piece of equipment or anything else for that matter, I let them resolve it themselves. The last thing I want to do is act like a referee." Jack, a production worker, agreed:

> We try to keep managers out of our affairs. You would have to be pretty stupid to get them involved. We had one new guy who went blabbing to [the team leader] about some problem he had and he found out real quick how we feel about that.

Finally, Bernie, an engineer, explains his views on submitting conflicts to supervisors: "You can't run to [the team leader] every time you are pissed at someone. That kind of kindergarten stuff just doesn't fly around here."

Despite these general sentiments, managers regularly intervene to help employees talk through their differences. Yet as Blackian theory predicts, superiors in this socially close environment usually limit their participation to a mediator role. Mediation attempts to repair relationships rather than end conflict by fiat or choosing a winner (Black and Baumgartner, 1983:100–102). Mediation at HelpCo is sometimes therapeutic as well: Both parties may be defined as suffering self-conflicts and in need of help.[6] Managers, for instance, may encourage individuals to discuss their problems with the hope they will discover and address the underlying sources of trouble. Christine, a team leader in repair, expresses a commonly held view: "I try to help people [work out differences] if they need it, but I don't like to pick sides. Often both people are right or have their own reasons for acting the way they do."

Mediation, therapeutic or otherwise, is found throughout the organization. Theresa, an accounting team leader, intervened in a conflict between a senior and junior bookkeeper over the former's tendency to "boss others around." Meeting in a conference room one morning, both sides explained their respective positions. Brenda, the junior employee, claimed that she felt uncomfortable with Stacy, her senior counterpart, "always looking over my shoulder." Stacy argued that Brenda overreacted and that she was just trying to help. According to Theresa, the meeting "cleared the air" between the two. Although the "hard feelings" did not entirely dissipate, Brenda and Stacy were able to work peacefully thereafter.

Conflict between lower ranking peers is also subject to mediation from time to time. Greg, a team leader in the production division, observed a conflict between Nick and Don, who were arguing over the proper method to assemble a small electronic device. After approaching the two parties, Greg convinced both to meet privately in his office to "have a cigarette and cool down." Although Nick and Don did not resolve their dispute during the meeting, they agreed not to let the conflict affect their working relationship. Greg played a minor role in the discussion, choosing instead to let Nick and Don do most of the talking. In another case occurring near the bottom of the hierarchy, Bobby, a team leader in shipping, acted as a mediator when Elaine complained that she was disturbed by the "aloofness" of Shannon, a coworker. Elaine first approached Bobby, who in turn talked to Shannon and then persuaded the two antagonists to meet in his office. During the meeting, Shannon "opened up," explaining that she was naturally shy rather than aloof. Elaine responded by claiming she would try to be tolerant of Shannon's idiosyncrasies. Although the relationship between the two parties improved after the meeting, they remained somewhat distant. Bobby, pleased with his role as mediator, noted that in order for Elaine and Shannon to work out their differences "they need to talk and get to know each other's personalities."

Conflict between managers is also regularly handled through mediation. Consider the case of Paul and Brian, team leaders in repair, who had several arguments, ostensibly about procedures for repairing a complex computer system. Their division leader,

Ralph, noticed the hostility between the two team leaders and spoke with each individually to get their versions of the quarrel. After doing so, Ralph determined that a host of underlying unresolved differences were responsible. In response, he suggested that Paul and Brian make a concerted effort to "get things out into the open." Paul took the initiative and managed to get Brian to hold a private meeting with Ralph acting as a mediator. According to Paul: "Even though we still disagree on a lot of stuff, we respect each other more. His attitude about me has changed [after the meeting], which makes it much easier for me to approach him and deal with [disagreements]."

If disputants are not part of the same department, both of their supervisors may act together to mediate the conflict. This happened in a dispute between Victor, an engineer, and Beth, a sales representative. Victor was angry at Beth for misleading a customer about the functioning of a popular product. Eric and Mike, the engineering and marketing directors, met with the two adversaries over lunch and together they discussed the issue at length. The conflict was determined to be the result of differences in perception. As Victor noted: "They [sales representatives] have a different mentality. They deal with clients all the time, and so they are able to perceive what the clients want. Then they tell them [clients] that we [engineers] can deliver, which isn't always the case. We can't just make anything they want." Victor and Beth agreed to meet regularly in the future in an attempt to make sure they were more aware of each other's "problems."

Hugh, the human relations director, played the role of mediator in a few disputes, all of which involved team leaders. In one case, two team leaders engaged in a protracted conflict over management styles. It began when, Bill, a repair team leader who had been with the company for three years, immediately took offense to the leadership technique of Stan, a newly hired team leader in shipping. Bill, who practiced a "hands-off" management style, was particularly offended with the more "hands-on, controlling" approach used by his fellow team leader. Bill made passing remarks to Stan on the shopfloor and in the lunchroom. At first, Stan politely ignored the remarks, but later began defending his management style. Eventually it got to the point that both parties would exchange nasty remarks every time they encountered one another. At the suggestion of Ollie, the director of operations, Hugh met with the team leaders in his office to discuss the dispute. Unable to make much progress, Hugh had Bill and Stan complete written personality tests similar to the one used by the firm when considering workers for promotion to supervisory positions. The results confirmed what each knew, that they had drastically different philosophies on how to manage people. Hugh concluded that it would best if Bill and Stan reduced contact in the future, which they have done successfully.

While HelpCo has no established public forums for the mediation of conflict, several formal attempts have been made to address ongoing disputes by bringing parties together. In one case, weekly meetings among selected members of the finance and operations departments were scheduled to help the two groups resolve a lingering conflict. The source of trouble was the untimely delivery of parts to the repair division. Purchasing clerks in the finance department claimed the repair workers were poor planners and therefore often made frantic, last-minute requests for parts. Frustrated with this pattern, several clerks purposely delayed movement of parts to the repair department "so the [repair] guys will learn to get their act together." After several weeks, Frank, the finance director, became aware of the problem and decided to hold a weekly meeting between the two groups to improve communication. This effort was considered effective. As Daryl, one of the repair workers, explained:

> [Before the meetings] there was no strong working relationship with us and purchasing. We would see them in the hall and say "hi," but that was it. When we had to deal with each other, we would just pass pieces of paper, but that doesn't carry any personality, any feeling with it. Now we have a better understanding of them and where they are coming from. So now even in problem situations, there is a connection, a link between us.

During the same period as the previous case, several repair team leaders were involved in a protracted dispute with two production team leaders over the priority of scarce parts. Like the preceding case, discord was interpreted as stemming from a communication problem. Here, Ollie, the director of operations, developed an "in-house" course designed to educate individuals in both departments about each other's work. It was never implemented, however, and according to several parties, the problem remains unresolved.

Executives also establish formal programs in an effort to restore harmony to their relationships. One such case originated when Pete, the president, became concerned with what he saw was the development of a "tribal mentality" among those in the executive ranks. He pointed to several recent director-level conflicts over jurisdictional issues. To deal with what he saw as a growing threat to HelpCo's unique organizational structure, Pete created a "facilitator" program. This program was designed to allow disputing directors to bring their conflicts to a fellow director for mediation. The practice was unpopular and was dropped less than six months after it was started. According to Frank, the director of finance, parties were reluctant to express their feelings to individuals not directly involved in the matter at hand. Still worried about the growth of myopic views, Pete decided to increase director interaction by having himself and fellow executives meet twice a week for lunch (in addition to their weekly staff meeting). He explained that this practice proved to be successful in getting directors to know each other's "needs" and forcing them to deal "openly" with conflicts that surface during the week. Changing the interaction among directors was therefore defined by Pete as having therapeutic value.

In recent years, HelpCo executives have also brought in "management consultants" to study and offer solutions to communication and other interpersonal and intrapersonal problems. These individuals, most of whom have advanced degrees in psychology or business, have administered attitude surveys to employees, held workshops to discuss "stress management," and developed "action plans" to create a "high-trust work culture." Similar practices designed to improve employee relations can be found elsewhere in corporate America (Kunda, 1992). "Sensitivity training" seminars, which teach employees to understand and respect racial and gender differences, are especially popular. Also common are "retreats," in which employees spend the weekend together away from the workplace and engage in various "team-building" exercises (Piombino, 1995). Academics are frequently hired as management consultants (Kunda, 1992:78, n. 16). Most consultants at HelpCo, for example, are on the faculty of the local university in either the business school or psychology department. They rely on a host of social scientific theories, many from a field known as "organizational behavior." From this perspective, employee conflict is viewed as an outgrowth of unhealthy individuals and relationships within organizations. Applied social science is therefore often a kind of therapy,[7] and accordingly it finds a receptive audience in the postbureaucratic organization.

Blackian theory predicts that subservient peers will act like children. Evidence shows that they do: Workers in hierarchical organizations hit each other, make threats, and engage in other punitive behavior, while their superiors attempt to pacify and adjudicate disputes. When hierarchy weakens, therapy and conciliation emerge. Peers in the therapeutic corporation thus help themselves and others address what are considered to be self-conflicts. They attempt to accommodate others as much as possible, but share their feelings if deemed necessary. Managers play a limited role, sometimes helping people work out their differences. But like social life in general, social control is decentralized. People handle conflict, including their intrapersonal troubles, similarly to how they conduct all of their business, with little interference from superiors.

# FIVE

# Therapeutic Protest

Although it may appear that social control is always downward or lateral, it is also directed up the organizational hierarchy. Inferiority can limit options, but people nonetheless define and respond to deviant conduct by their superiors in various ways (Baumgartner, 1984). Employees may, for example, complain to coworkers, steal and destroy company property, file lawsuits, go on strike, or resign. People in the therapeutic corporation, by contrast, normally help superiors overcome their alleged problems rather than punish them for behaving improperly. Yet therapy from below is more restrained and private than when initiated from above or by peers.

## Upward Conflict

Upward conflict occurs when a subordinate disapproves of the conduct of a superior. Inequality and social distance produce *rebellion*, a punitive mode of upward social control (Black, 1990:47–49). Rebellion mirrors discipline to some degree (Baumgartner, 1984:336; Black, 1990:47–49), but it is more covert and less formal (Black, 1993:150,153). Blackian theory predicts that rebellion will be most destructive when inferiority and social remoteness are extreme (Black, 1990:47–49, 1993: 154).[1] Rebellion should accordingly weaken and become less frequent when subordinates and superiors move closer to each other. At the smallest distances in vertical, cultural and relational, space, remedial social control, including therapy, should appear.

Evidence from rigidly hierarchical and socially segregated work settings, especially those of the past, shows that rebellion is strong and often collective (Black, 1990:47–49; see also Senechal de la Roche, 1996:112). Below we see, too, that rebellion is weak and individualized in organizations with more moderate levels of inequality and social distance. Also consistent with Blackian theory, subordinates at HelpCo and in other decentralized communal environments most often attempt to help rather than hurt their superiors. Much of this help is covert. Subordinates secretly diagnose managers and often disguise their attempts to help. Superiors also solicit assistance from below, but subordinates are not called on, nor do they seek to counsel or otherwise work through problems with managers.[2] Moreover, superiors sometimes turn the tables and define subordinates who directly express their concerns as having problems themselves.

### Strong Rebellion

When inequality and social distance are great, rebellion is potent and frequently organized. Consider slave laborers. Working under conditions of extreme subordination and social segregation, slaves seek revenge against owners violently and collectively. On Brazilian slave plantations in the nineteenth-century, for example, destruction of property and infliction of physical harm were common methods of protest. One indication of the intensity of rebellion in this setting was the extent to which plantation owners sought to protect themselves. Owners and members of their families were especially worried about being poisoned by slaves. Local druggists were made aware of such concerns: "[Druggists] had to be extremely careful that prescriptions to be picked up by slaves could not be opened without breaking the seal, for the slaves were masters in the art of herbal poisons and vengeful enough to seize the opportunity" (Dean, 1976:85). Aware of the dangers surrounding them, plantation owners kept large dogs by their sides and many hired armed guards to protect themselves. Planters were particularly concerned about slaves banding together and initiating direct attacks. To avert this possibility, rest periods were staggered so that slaves would not all be idle at the same time. Noting the radical lengths that owners went to thwart slave reprisals, some observers described them as suffering from "planter's paranoia." (Dean, 1976:85).

In the mines of southern Rhodesia earlier this century, where black workers labored in slave-like conditions, attacks on mine property, including the burning of thatch roof huts and the maiming of cattle, were used to collectively strike back at mine owners (van Onselen, 1976:242). Other forms of protest were less aggressive, examples of what Baumgartner (1984:308–312) calls "covert retaliation." But these actions were nonetheless designed to punish white mine owners and managers:

> Daily, hundreds of crimes were committed on the mining properties with the specific goal of rectifying the balance between employees and their employers. African workers constantly pilfered small items of mine stores—such as candles—or helped themselves to substantial quantities of detonators and dynamite which they used for fishing. Wage rates were altered on documents, and hundreds of work . . . tickets were forged by miners who sought to gain compensation for what they had been denied through the system. (van Onselen, 1976:240)

Workers also feigned illness, injured themselves, and were careless with equipment, causing it to break.

Strong rebellion is common as well in factory regimes with rigid hierarchies and large social gaps between superiors and subordinates. Peasants working in the factories of precommunist Russia at the end of the nineteenth century engaged in a series of strikes ranging "from isolated spontaneous outbursts of rage against low wages, fines, living conditions, illegal firings, and other abuses, to longer and more organized protests demanding substantive changes in industrial relations" (Glickman, 1984:20). Some of these actions were violent. In one case, several hundred, mostly women, weavers, upset with verbal insults and sexual intimidation, joined together and invaded a factory office and destroyed furniture, record books, and other company property: "They then moved on to the company store, which they looted and destroyed. They invaded the weaving department and wrecked the looms. Finally, they went in search of the factory director and, not finding him on the premises, went to his house with the intention of killing him" (Glickman, 1984:166). The director escaped physical harm, but the strike lasted over a week.

High levels of inequality and social distance also characterized early American factories. According to one observer, American auto companies were run by "industrial despots acting like feudal lords" (Gartman, 1986:183–84). In this kind of setting, workers frequently attempt to harm organizations and their representatives. At the Lincoln Motor Company,

> [m]ishaps—whether caused by sabotage or carelessness—occurred constantly. Machines would be thrown out of adjustment overnight so that the operation next morning might go on for hours turning out scrap before inspection could catch it. Screws were loosened, bolts were removed which could allow parts to fall and be damaged. Loose nuts were found in crankcases of engines, feed pipes were plugged. On one occasion, cans full of powder were found in the coal supply, and fire extinguishers were plugged with cotton. (Leland, 1966:187; quoted in Gartman, 1986: 171)

At Keim Mills, a company that produced automobile parts, aggrieved workers occasionally engaged in fist fights with some of the more antagonistic foremen (Gartman, 1986:184).

Migrant workers labor in conditions of considerable vertical, relational, and cultural distance. Rebellion is correspondingly violent and frequently collective. Earlier this century, migrant agricultural workers from Eastern Europe, though sometimes using flight to express their displeasure with working conditions, regularly rebelled against their superiors. In the Prussian province of Saxony, for example, several workers in 1908 walked off an agricultural work site and threatened to kill the foreman. Armed with hoes, spades, and stones, they clashed with the police before surrendering (Müller, 1991:87). In 1911, striking workers "smashed the windows at the flat of their foreman in protest against discriminatory work and living conditions." (Müller, 1991:87).

When socially distant subordinates have potential supporters who are close to them—vertically, culturally and relationally—but distant from superiors, the likelihood of collective rebellion is especially great (see Black, 1993:131–132).[3] This pattern was evident among peasant laborers in southeastern Italy at the start of the twentieth century:

> The gang system itself favored the development of class solidarity. Large groups of men working together for weeks at time shared ideas, experiences, and information. Furthermore, there was no divisive job stratification. . . . Within the gang assigned to a particular job there was no hierarchy according to skill, diligence, or seniority. All were treated as unskilled and sometimes anonymous field hands working at the same task for the same money. . . . Under such conditions, it was a small step for the labourers to view their plight as a collective one. (Snowden, 1986:23–24)

Rebellion was consequently strong and organized.

Changes in hierarchy and relations among workers themselves also explain the rise of collective rebellion early this century in the American workplace and its gradual decline starting at the middle of the century. In the small shops of the late nineteenth century, for example, relationships were hierarchical but socially close, and union formation was uncommon:

> The personal ties that owners of small businesses established with workers in many cases tended to obscure . . . class differences between them. Loyalty had a direct and personal meaning for workers, and many were reluctant to break the bonds it formed. At McCormick, for example, the company could count on some employees to side with

it rather than union organizers; this divided the workforce and prevented unionization. (Edwards, 1979:27)

The successive escalation of organized rebellion in large factories followed the growing relational and cultural separation of workers from owners:

> Only later, when the workforce had grown far beyond the size at which personal ties to the entrepreneur could be important, did workers organize successfully. And at Pabst, despite exceptionally long hours, no successful organizing drive was possible until the class differences— so long hidden by friendships, common German heritage, and other personal bonds—were at last exposed so clearly that they could not be ignored. (Edwards, 1979:27)

Toward the middle of the twentieth century, larger enterprises began embracing organizational structures that stratified and differentiated workers. In these kinds of enterprises, subordinates compete with one another for positions on the corporate ladder. "The workers' response . . . has resulted primarily in individual and small-group discontent rather than in collective action. . . . [The] stratification and redivision of workers make collective action more difficult" (Edwards, 1979: 154).

Allies need not be fellow workers. Subordinates in some settings can count on the support of family, friends, and others to help pursue upward conflict. With lots of potential partisans available, rebellion can be quite potent. Individuals employed in the transport industry of early twentieth-century northern China, who worked under the unyielding authority of guild bosses, had strong kinship ties that could be summoned at virtually any time. Grievances against bosses were often expressed in a violent manner, frequently with the assistance of kin:

> The 1935 case of transport worker Su Zhenbao is typical of a worker-boss conflict. Laid off by a foreman named Yu for a trivial offense, Su went to Yu's house with a wooden club and assaulted him. Two of Yu's nephews, as well as Su's brother, jumped into the fray, and Su bit a large chuck out of Yu's hand. Yu was luckier than Yang Derun, one of Tianjin's most famous transport guild bosses. One

of Yang's workers, angry at being cheated out of his fair share of pay, got into an argument with Yang and stabbed him six times in the head and once in the chest. . . . Another boss, who made what his employees regarded as excessive deductions from their pay, was assaulted by a group of them and beaten. (Hershatter, 1986:135)

Contemporary multinational corporations often locate in underdeveloped countries and hire members of indigenous populations to work in factories. In these settings, the vertical, cultural, and relational gaps between managers and workers are great. The local workforce may also have strong ties to the larger community. If so, conditions are ripe for collective rebellion. This is the case at foreign-owned manufacturing plants in Malaysia. Here, young female workers and their supporters retaliate in various ways against company property and managers. An observer in the mid-1970s noted that sometimes

subversive acts were spontaneous, carried out by individual workers independently of each other. . . . When production targets seemed unbearable, or a foreman had been especially harsh, operators registered their private vengeance by damaging the very components they had painstakenly assembled. (Ong, 1987:210–11)

In other circumstances, local young men sympathetic to the plight of workers would attack misbehaving foremen:

In 1976, an Indian foreman was set upon, "beaten and badly hurt on the face and stomach by an unknown gang" according to [company] records. A Malay assistant foreman coming to his aid was also beaten up. According to an informal questioning of workers, the foreman deserved punishment because he refused workers their 15 minute breaks, insulted them about personal matters, followed women into the locker room, and threatened to terminate their employment whenever he felt necessary. He became blacklisted among village youths. (Ong, 1987:211)

A Chinese foreman was beaten by locals for dating an operator, a practice that violated a warning by the community that sexual encounters with young women working on the line were forbidden (Ong, 1987:213). Moreover, "[t]here had been at least two other incidents of nocturnal attacks on male workers—none of local origin—outside the [company] gates" (Ong, 1987: 212).

Employees in the modern American workplace have few external allies. High rates of geographic mobility mean people are unlikely to have extended family members or others partisan enough to help pursue workplace grievances.[4] Employees are also less apt to receive support from local, regional, or national labor organizations. Union membership is on a steady decline—for example, whereas more than 35 percent of American workers belonged to labor unions in 1945 (U.S. Bureau of the Census, 1975), less than 15 percent of the workforce is currently unionized (U.S. Department of Labor, 1996).

But employees have a source of support mostly unavailable in the past: the state. Although the government theoretically plays a nonpartisan settlement role in conflict, it often takes sides (Black, 1993:139). Black shows how legal partisanship follows the same principles as other support behavior, meaning the government is most likely to favor higher-status parties (1993:139–140; see generally, Black, 1976:ch. 2). Thus, the state has historically sided with employers in labor-management conflict. Local governments, for example, often supplied police officers to help early American firms counter striking workers (Brecher, 1972). Today, however, employees can sometimes count on the government for support. In the United States, several administrative agencies offer legal assistance to workers who have complaints against corporations. The Equal Employment Opportunity Commission is one of the most active federal agencies, initiating criminal action and filing lawsuits on behalf of employees discriminated or harassed on the job "because of race, color, sex, religion, national origin, or age" (Rapoport and Zevnik, 1989:271). The jurisdiction of administrative agencies is expanding, meaning upward social control could take a new shape in the future. Rather than turning to their family, community, or union for assistance, workers who have grievances against their employers may increasingly call on the government. Yet the state is not always accessible, and workers are frequently on their own. Rebellion in modern organizations is therefore weak.

## Weak Rebellion

As inequality and social distance between superiors and subordinates decline, rebellion becomes less common and less potent. This is the case with operations workers at HelpCo, who are subject to moderate levels of subordination. Rebellion, while uncommon overall, is almost always initiated by individuals acting alone. HelpCo has thus never experienced a labor strike or organized work slowdown.[5]

Individuals can rebel by suing or threatening to sue the company.[6] Although no lawsuits were initiated by HelpCo employees, one individual threatened legal action. Helen, a new production worker, planned to file a sexual discrimination lawsuit after receiving a written warning for several unexcused absences. Hugh, the human relations director, first became aware of the potential suit when Helen's lawyer mailed a letter to the firm describing her grievance. The company's response was swift. Hugh discovered that Helen had told some of her coworkers about an unsuccessful attempt to sue her previous employer for similar reasons. Believing this fact showed Helen's present claim had no merit, Hugh began building a case. He documented virtually everything Helen did, focusing on the time she arrived in the mornings and how many days she missed work altogether. Several weeks after her lawyer's letter arrived at HelpCo, Helen was confronted with evidence showing her poor performance. She resigned shortly afterwards. Two years earlier, a shipping clerk had mentioned to a coworker that he was considering a lawsuit against the company for managerial "favoritism." The clerk's team leader was not aware of his intentions, and, according to the coworker, the aggrieved clerk dropped the issue when he transferred to another team.

The most notable case of rebellion at HelpCo was more symbolic than destructive. Dennis, a shipping employee, caused a stir when he periodically urinated on the floor of the men's bathroom adjacent to the operations department. During the three-month period in which this activity occurred, the identity of the so-called "phantom pisser" was unknown. Dennis was not connected to the behavior until it stopped immediately after he resigned. This behavior was by most accounts an act of rebellion. According to Jenny, his team leader, Dennis appeared to have problems with her leadership style he was unwilling to discuss. His behavior, therefore, could be considered a response to a grievance.[7]

Other social scientists have documented how the company restroom can serve as a location for individuals to protest managerial action. At a contemporary British manufacturing plant, for example, workers use the "loo" (toilet) as a place to express their grievances: "The widespread shopfloor view of the toilet as a collusive retreat was discernible on its walls that were covered in a 'graffiti of resistance'; a typical comment was 'Evans (the superintendent) is a cunt' " (Collinson, 1992:137). Employees in a large American factory retreat to the bathroom to get away from the rigors of the shopfloor and its overbearing foremen. Besides being a venue to complain about managers, the toilet provides a safe place read the newspaper and violate the unpopular no smoking policy: "[I]n the men's bathroom, there are times during the day when you are in big trouble if you need a stall. You have to wait, listening to the rustling of paper, and watching smoke roll over the closed stall door" (Balzer, 1976: 86). Consistent with Blackian theory, individual rebellion of this kind is typically found in bureaucratically organized factory settings, where inequality and social distance are present in moderate degrees.

No physical attacks against superiors were documented at HelpCo during this study. Several years earlier, a male production employee who had been formally reprimanded for poor performance kicked in the door of a team leader and screamed obscenities. The angry worker quickly departed the plant and never returned. Current managers do not consider violent retaliation a serious possibility. The only exception is Steve, the shipping division leader. He previously worked at a steel plant in the northeastern United States and had experiences with workers physically threatening superiors. Steve currently has an unlisted home phone number because, as he said, laughing: "Just in case I have to let someone go and they don't agree with my decision." It is not coincidental that the one instance of near violence aimed at a supervisor took place in the production division. Likewise, it is not surprising that Steve, who has an unlisted phone number because of concern about violent rebellion, supervises workers in the operations department. The distance between subordinates and superiors is greater than elsewhere in the firm. Violence is unthinkable for professionals, who work under weak hierarchies and are socially close to their managers.

Superiors may actively attempt to reduce the social gap between themselves and subordinates, and in turn lessen the possibility of rebellion. One team leader at HelpCo mentioned the importance of "hanging out with the guys" on the production line and letting them know that he "is not the boss." Another regularly took his team to a local bar to "keep open lines of communication." Both team leaders claimed that workers under their command were likely to approach them and openly discuss their grievances rather than express them in less acceptable covert outlets.

This same pattern is found in other organizations. Consider longshoremen on the northwestern coast of the United States:

> Few of the foremen ever attempt to assume any role than that of "one of the boys," and those who maintain themselves as part of the longshore in-group enjoy a good deal of popularity among the men and maintain good production records, because the longshoremen will usually give a break to a foreman who maintains his status as one of the men. (Pilcher, 1972:99)

According to a recent study of American labor-management conflict, "Going out for a beer symbolizes status equality, as does the common use of 'shop talk' and a linguistic style that includes 'cussing' like a 'normal guy' " (Friedman, 1992:152). When managers and workers share social experiences, they are able to develop "private understandings of each other" and handle their differences in less adversarial ways (Friedman, 1992:150–151).

Drinking together, in particular, can play a key role in weakening hierarchy and social distance, even if only temporarily:

"The raising of the first glass, bottle, aluminum can, or paper cup is a sign that participants may take to mean a relaxation of ordinary work rules" (Van Maanen, 1992:39). The contemporary "office party" is a setting where workers and managers frequently socialize and share grievances. In London's Metropolitan Police Department,

> the office party allows for some often blunt discourse across . . . ranks. With alcohol obvious and everyone drunk, an officer is not responsible for what he says and does. Higher officials can criticize lower ones, and, more important, lower ones can "come on about their complaints" with the higher ranks. (Van Maanen, 1992:49)

Other events where drinking is prominent, such as "pub crawls," are also valued by police officers for their "tension-relieving" effects. In Japanese corporations, "office parties with dinner and drinks permit the subordinates to adopt the guise of mild inebriation" and openly voice their complaints to managers (Ouchi, 1981:45). An anthropologist studying a large Japanese bank noted that "[t]he gesture of filling another's glass is a convenient bridge across strained relationships" (Rohlen, 1974:109). Golf outings, which are quite popular in Japan, also provide employees an opportunity to break down social barriers: "At these times subordinates can feel free to ask questions and raise objections suppressed in the office and expect the boss to respond sympathetically" (Ouchi, 1981:45).

## Therapy from Below

When inequality and social distance are minimal, rebellion disappears and subordinates are likely to engage in upward therapy. Misbehaving superiors are no longer enemies to be punished but victims needing help overcoming their problems. Subordinates are likely to secretly *evaluate superiors*, often with the assistance of coworkers, and diagnose their condition. They also attempt to *induce change* by adjusting their behavior and forcing managers to reflect on and ultimately change themselves. Subordinates may *open up* and offer direct help, usually after managers seek their assistance. These strategies are found throughout HelpCo and in other work settings where people are socially close.

## Evaluating Superiors

HelpCo employees often share their upward conflicts with others, usually coworkers, and engage in what is commonly called gossip. As social control, gossip involves aggrieved parties evaluating the conduct of a party not present (Black, 1995:855, n. 129; see also Gluckman, 1963; Merry, 1984). It is like a "trial in absentia" (Black, 1989:76). Gossip is common among subordinates in work settings of all kinds. Young part-time workers in modern America, for instance, share many of their grievances against managers with fellow employees (Tucker, 1993:30–32). At HelpCo, gossip is most concerned with trying to comprehend the behavior of others, in a therapeutic spirit, than with passing judgment. So in the postbureaucratic setting, gossip is like a psychiatric evaluation in absentia. When managers are evaluated and diagnosed in this manner, they are assumed to be suffering from self-conflicts and not entirely responsible for their behavior.

People's personalities and backgrounds are especially likely to be the source of therapeutic gossip. This was the case when Barbara, an accounting team leader, raised her voice at Stacy, a junior accountant. Following the incident, Stacy immediately told several coworkers about it. One of her peers, Brenda, mentioned that she had a similar experience in the recent past and suggested it might have been because Barbara was new on the job and had no leadership background. After reflecting on the matter for two days, Stacy accepted this assessment and decided to give Barbara a "second chance."

Another case of therapeutic gossip was initiated by Todd, an engineer, who objected to his team leader Jeff's decision to modify the design of a new product without notifying anyone. Upon discovering this, Todd informed a close coworker, who suggested that Jeff's youth and inexperience in managing people may be responsible for his actions. Todd agreed and decided not to confront the leader with his concerns because, in his words: "the project was almost completed and I knew he [Jeff] would be reassigned and will probably learn how to manage people as he gets more experience."

Seemingly minor incidents can lead to therapeutic gossip. In one case, for example, Dean complained to Charlie, a fellow production team leader, about their division leader Patrick's habit of smoking cigarettes in the presence of others without asking permission. Following some discussion, Dean and Charlie determined that trying to change Steve's behavior would be pointless. Dean noted:

> If I told him not to smoke around me, he'd never come to my office. So I deal with it. I don't think he realizes it bothers us. He's older than a lot of us and not so much concerned with his health. Smoking is almost natural for people in his generation.

In another case, Stan consulted coworkers and concluded the following about his sometimes "overbearing" manager Steve:

> He [Steve] occasionally gets off on this power trip. He tries to assert himself. I guess it's because before he came here he had worked in more rigid environments where people's responsibilities were real clear-cut. Most of us are younger and don't like structure.

The conduct of top management also comes under scrutiny and is frequently subject to therapeutic gossip. A number of employees throughout the firm, for example, objected to an executive decision to change the policy on stock ownership. The new policy required employees to wait two years after they leave the firm to cash in their shares. This decision was described by Richard, an accountant, as a reflection of executive "paranoia" caused by a recent slowdown in business. Here, a personality disorder was assigned to management as a whole. Pete, the company president, is not immune to gossip. Several repair team leaders gossiped about Pete when he hesitated to go along with their suggestion to reorganize the repair department. The leaders centered their discussion on his "overly diplomatic" management style. Christine, a repair team leader, described Pete's personality:

[He] tries to make everyone happy. He's very open, a good-natured guy who will make you feel good while you're talking to him, but you can't expect him to give you a definitive answer on anything. Of course, that's probably how he got to be president—by not offending anyone.

The concern again was with trying to analyze and understand the motivation behind a superior's deviant actions.

Some of those in leadership positions are aware that they are being informally diagnosed, via gossip, by subordinates. A few, including Joe, a production team leader, see it as potentially harmful:

Rumors spread like wildfire around here. Sometimes it involves harmless stuff about who is sleeping with whom. But other times it is dangerous. Just last week someone started a rumor about a wage freeze. It wasn't true, but a lot of people believed it, and if it would have gotten out of hand, it could really hurt morale.

Most supervisors, however, see some therapeutic value in gossip. As Hank, an engineering team leader, claimed: "Sometimes we [supervisors] hear things through the grapevine that we need to hear about, like how people are doing, how they are feeling."

Managers are also inclined to take what they regard as helpful action in response to gossip. Ralph, the repair division leader, discovered that those under his direction were frustrated with his inability to communicate effectively. He then engaged in self-reflection: "I have a feeling they [subordinates] are not entirely happy with my style, and they are probably hesitant about telling me. I think I give off this aura that I'm not very open, but that is something I'm working on now, trying to change." The executives (the department directors) respond to gossip as well. In one case, they changed the location of their yearly weekend "retreat" from an exclusive mountain resort to a local hotel. This decision came after executives learned through the gossip network that many employees did not approve of top management "wasting" company funds. The director of finance was especially concerned about top management's alleged "insensitivity." During the retreat, executives participated in an exercise in self-criticism coordinated by Hugh, the director of human relations.

### Inducing Change

A more direct, though still largely covert, strategy of upward therapy has subordinates disguising their attempts to help by making adjustments in their behavior so that superiors are forced to recognize and address their intrapersonal problems. This strategy is somewhat coercive, but ultimately therapeutic: Managers are considered to be experiencing self-conflicts and needing assistance in returning to normality. In Japanese corporations, workers frequently disguise their grievances:

> [T]he individual unhappy with his boss or with relationships in the group is likely to set himself at odds with group norms where matters of personal preference intersect. Wearing excessive makeup, drinking too much, joining a leftist youth group, avoiding office social activities, and remaining notably silent during discussions are examples. (Rohlen, 1974:111–112)

Though Japanese managers occasionally reflect on and modify their own conduct, they are more likely to respond therapeutically to the actions of subordinates:

> The understanding is that resistance is analogous to the rebellious behavior of children toward their families. The individual's natural state of existence, it is assumed, is within some group, and resistance is interpreted as essentially a sign of unhappiness and personal need. Thus, with few exceptions, acts of nonconformity are answered with sympathy and with special efforts to bring the individual back into the fold. (Rohlen, 1974:112)

A similar pattern is found in bureaucratic settings where superiors and subordinates are socially close. A sociologist examining life inside a large American corporation discovered that "many secretaries turn[ed] to classical ways members of the subordinate class manage to get what they want from the more powerful: through assumed helplessness and emotional manipulation" (Kanter, 1977:96). While the traditional boss-secretary relationship is stratified in terms of authority and financial rewards, it contains a considerable degree of intimacy. It thus differs from many hierarchical relationships, where superiors and subordinates are socially distant. The presence of intimacy promotes social control that is coercive but that elicits a therapeutic response from above.[8]

At HelpCo, workers induce change in several ways. One way of getting the attention of managers is to disregard their authority. Consider the case of Mike, the marketing director, who modified his behavior after several sales representatives chose to recognize a coworker as their boss. Not long after being hired, Mike angered most of the sales force with his authoritarian attitude. Ann, who was especially irritated, explains what she believed to be the source of Mike's problem:

> He [Mike] has a different management style. Now I understand where he is coming from. He's an old-order auto executive from Detroit. So he's from the school that says "My God, I'm the director and when I say something, that's it." It's almost like a Theory X management style as opposed to the way we are around here. We are very, very informal and unstructured, pretty much a Theory Y style, or even Z. And that's created a tremendous personality conflict in the whole department. Everybody had a difficult time dealing with him. We aren't used to people telling us what to do.[9]

Ann and her peers responded to their dissatisfaction by "cutting him out of the loop," while David, a senior sales rep, performed most the activities formally under the jurisdiction of the director. Mike eventually came to realize he was being ignored and has gradually gained respect from most of his subordinates as he learned to compromise. He has not changed completely, however. As David noted:

> He still makes little snide remarks over the telephone [when talking to sales reps] that hurt the feelings of some people. [He] questions their ability or commitment to the

job. I believe he does it as a way to motivate people, but I really don't think he realizes his effect on people.

Employees may be rather creative when attempting to help managers. Members of a repair team were especially clever in responding to their team leader Frank's alleged deficiencies as a manager. In this case, Roger, one of the senior repair workers, noticed that coworker Luke was "cherry-picking," a practice that involves purposely selecting products that are easy to repair. This practice violates an informal policy of randomly choosing pieces of equipment to repair as they arrive at the plant. Because Luke chose the easiest jobs, he could work at a rapid pace and his performance appeared superior to other members of the team. Rather than confront Luke, Roger and other team members determined that Frank's "meek management style" was responsible for him not addressing the problem. After several weeks, the workers began restricting their output, hoping this would cause Frank to take notice. Observing a change in his team's behavior, Frank suspected the new employee was negatively affecting the group, although he was not sure why. Frank then monitored Luke for just over a week and eventually approached him. Embarrassed, Luke resigned shortly after being confronted. The remaining members of the team continue to be concerned about Frank's management skills.

Similarly, members of a production team sought to induce change after their team leader Charlie hired Bert, a young man whom many workers considered unqualified. Most team members believed Bert was given the position solely because of a prior friendship with Charlie. When Charlie neglected to address Bert's poor performance, the production workers decided to "send a message" to Charlie by nominating Bert for an "employee of the year" award. After discovering what happened, Charlie interpreted the team members' actions therapeutically as a "cry for help." He concluded that he needed to get more involved in the affairs of his subordinates so, in Charlie's words, "I can know what's on their minds and how they are feeling." Charlie has tried to change his relationship with the team by regularly meeting with members. He also administers a monthly survey that encourages employees to express in writing their attitudes about the department and offer suggestions for improvement. According to Alex, a team member, these efforts have been largely successful, although many people still believe Charlie needs to work on his "personal relationship skills."

A more drastic and permanent mode of inducement is resignation. An accountant, for example, resigned after concluding that she and her team leader had irreconcilable differences: "We get along okay outside of work. We are actually friends. But as [fellow] workers, we are a mismatch. She isn't my idea of a good leader. She doesn't trust the people she works with." Quitting, in this instance, was defined as helping the manager realize her problem. Most departures at HelpCo are amicable like this case. One exception involved a woman in production who left the firm one morning and never returned after discovering she had not received a promised pay raise.

### Opening Up

Managers in the therapeutic corporation also actively solicit help from below by encouraging subordinates to open up. Rather than counsel or directly help those higher in status, subordinates only offer advice. Moreover, they frequently find that managers dismiss their attempts to help or respond therapeutically themselves to advice coming from below.

Managers sometimes approach employees informally during the workday and ask for assistance. Carrie, an accountant, and Peggy, her team leader, were the participants in a typical case. Concerned that she had lost the respect of her team, Peggy met with Carrie during a lunch break. Carrie told Peggy that her management style was becoming too authoritarian and that this made her feel like a child. Peggy was surprised that she was perceived in this way, but agreed to spend less time monitoring Carrie and her coworkers. Another illustrative case began when Frank, who sensed he was losing his effectiveness as a repair division team leader, approached Roger, one of the more senior repair workers, for help. Roger politely told Frank he was "out of touch with the needs of the department." A recent decision to purchase an expensive computer system without asking his team members was cited by Roger as an indication of Frank's self-absorption. Frank saw the issue differently and described what he thought were the motivations behind Roger's comments:

> He [Roger] had good intentions. But he and [other workers] need to realize they can't be involved in every decision we [supervisors] make. We have to do things that aren't immediately popular, but that are in the long-term interest of the company. We need to make sure people are comfortable with that. If we aren't, then it's something we need to work on.

In this case both the manager and subordinate "worked on" their alleged problems with the self.

Managers are also sought out for help by *their* superiors. In these cases, occurring at higher social elevations, lower-ranking managers may act somewhat forcefully. In one such case, Patrick, the production division leader, became concerned that Ollie, the director of operations, was "losing touch" with the realities of business. One afternoon, after discovering that Ollie had unilaterally approved the modification of a popular HelpCo product, Patrick visited Ollie's office and explained that what may seem like minor changes from a distance can be very disruptive to workers on the line. Although according to Patrick it took several days to "sink in," Ollie promised to "get in the trenches" more often to better understand "what's really going on."

Pete, the president, is especially concerned with how he is perceived by others and frequently solicits input from others. He is particularly fond of walking around the plant and talking to people while they are working. Not all employees feel comfortable honestly expressing their opinions to Pete. Yet even production workers have spoken up on occasion. A policy change in the employee ownership plan and the purchase of a $100,000 computer were two decisions that generated much discussion on the production line. In addition, Bernie, an engineer, objected to a new product line being considered by the president and the department directors, while Scott, a sales representative, voiced his disapproval with a decision to cut back the per diem expenses in the marketing department. In these cases and several others, employees were frustrated with Pete's preference for diplomacy instead of action. This observation is consistent with the earlier comment about Pete's alleged tendency to smooth over problems. Rather than view his actions as malicious, however, employees attribute his behavior to an underlying personality trait.

Besides offering assistance informally, employees have access to a formal system that encourages them to comment on the behavior of management and offer helpful suggestions. According to Frank, the director of finance, this system, called *Open Up*,[10] is valuable: "Some people are just shy and need an outlet to express themselves." *Open Up* accepts written submissions (often anonymous) from individuals who comment on particular managerial decisions or supervisory behavior in general. Each week, a group of managers meets and prepares written answers to the questions, a practice that may involve gathering information from other individuals throughout the company. The responses are placed in a notebook, which is kept in the lunchroom.[11]

About two *Open Up* suggestions a week were offered during the nine-month research period. In one illustrative case, a production worker commented on an advertisement he had seen in an electronic trade magazine. The ad, partially paid for by HelpCo, congratulated one of the firm's most important lobbying groups on its fortieth anniversary. The worker questioned why the company had "wasted" money on what was believed to be an unnecessary advertisement.[12] Walter, the marketing team leader who had placed the advertisement, wrote a lengthy response justifying why the company places ads of that type. According to Walter, the response was aimed at getting the worker to "understand the bigger picture, to get a feel for what other people do and why they do what they do." Walter claimed that he is partly to blame and should do a better job educating workers about the nature of commerce.

In another written comment to *Open Up*, a worker questioned a decision made by Patrick, the production division manager, to reorganize part of the operations department. The employee was particularly concerned that people had been assigned a new team leader without being consulted beforehand. The author of the written comment suggested that this type of action is bad for employee morale and could cause people to leave the firm. The response, prepared by several department directors and division leaders, was filled with therapeutic language. It began as follows: "Personal anxiety is common when a number of changes occur in a relatively short period of time. We try to treat everyone fairly, but despite our best efforts someone is usually hurt." The managers listed several reasons that the reorganization was beneficial. They concluded by promising to change their management style and allow more employee influence over future decisions of this kind.

A third case followed a similar therapeutic logic. Alleged favoritism by Thomas, a recently hired production team leader, was the issue that initiated an *Open Up* comment. The concerned employee described how Thomas had immediately befriended two employees and had given them preference in selecting job assignments. The written response, prepared by Ollie, the director of operations, suggested the employee give Thomas a chance to "feel his way around and get to know everyone before confronting him with your complaint." Ollie spoke of this incident later and conceded that top management can get so "wrapped up in their own little worlds" that they become insensitive to the needs of others.

As the previous cases illustrate, exchanges in the *Open Up* system typically have a therapeutic focus. When voicing their concerns with management, individuals often claim that their superiors have attitude and general personality problems that can get in the way of healthy work relationships. For their part, managers view employee comments in a similar way. Consider the following comment submitted to *Open Up*: "I think the leaders [in this company] have their own problems when 99 percent of the [*Open Up*] complaints are seen as attitude problems." This remark reflects the ubiquitous and often reciprocal nature of therapy in the postbureaucratic organization.

Blackian theory predicts that rebellion thrives under conditions of inequality and social distance. Large gaps between superiors and subordinates produce violent attacks on employers and their representatives, destruction and appropriation of property, and threats of various kinds. But life in a therapeutic corporation is different. When vertical, cultural, and relational distance are small, rebellion recedes and upward therapy emerges. Managers are secretly diagnosed and induced to help themselves, while regularly turning to subordinates for advice on how to address what are considered to be their self-conflicts. Superiors no longer fear for their physical safety or worry about their property. Instead, the targets are their minds.

# SIX

# Conclusion

We have seen that therapy does not merely occur in the offices of psychiatrists and the wards of mental hospitals. It also occurs in the workplace. Therapy is especially active in the postbureaucratic organization, where people up and down the hierarchy diagnose and treat each other for various intrapersonal problems. While therapy among employees is informal and often quite mild, the particular form it takes depends on its direction. Downward therapy is the most forceful. Besides encouraging people to help themselves, superiors counsel subordinates and modify their work surroundings. Lateral therapy is frequently combined with conciliation. Peers accommodate each other as much as possible, but also share their thoughts as a means of helping themselves and others. Managers sometimes intervene and help peers restore harmony to their relationships. Upward therapy is mostly covert. Subordinates secretly evaluate and indirectly attempt to help superiors, and occasionally open up and offer direct advice.

All of the above contrasts drastically with settings such as slave plantations, serf estates, colonial work camps, and early factories—all settings with high levels of inequality and social distance. Where these conditions prevail, superiors readily punish subordinates by beating and fining them, restricting their privileges, and terminating them. Peers threaten and humiliate each other, make threats, and engage in fist fights before having their conflicts settled by fiat from above. Subordinates appropriate property, destroy equipment, and physically attack superiors. In contemporary bureaucratic firms, where inequality and social distance are present to a moderate degree, we find less potent forms of discipline, vengeance, settlement, and rebellion.

Donald Black's general theory of conflict explains these patterns: Different social structures attract different forms of social control. With vertical, cultural, and relational distance come judgment, condemnation, coercion, and punishment. Reduce these distances so that individuals are equal, homogeneous, and intimate, and social control becomes remedial. Instead of making people suffer for their mistakes, a central focus is helping them address their self-conflicts. The postbureaucratic organization, where most relationships span short distances in social space, is therefore a fertile environment for therapy.

Organizations in modern life come in a variety of shapes and sizes, and social control varies accordingly (Morrill, 1995:228). Yet long-term trends suggest that work settings will increasingly resemble the postbureaucratic organization. The wide social gaps found in organizations of the past are shrinking. If this continues, authoritative and partisan social control should further decline and therapy become more commonplace. This forecast contradicts a widespread view that the development of democracy in organizations necessitates a system of social control resembling law. However, such a forecast is entirely consistent with what we know about the social structure of therapy.

The conditions supporting therapy are also increasingly found beyond the workplace. A larger therapeutic order is therefore emerging in which people in families, schools, and other groups are defined as having problems with themselves rather than with others. This means that whereas moralism is weakening, conflict is not disappearing. It is becoming internalized.

## Therapeutic Democracy

A popular thesis claims that organizational democracy requires law-like measures for governing internal social relations, including the handling of conflict (e.g., Selznick, 1969; Bernstein, 1982). The main finding of this book challenges this view. Rather than achieving uniform treatment across cases, the overriding concern in the postbureaucratic organization (where relationships are relatively democratic) is helping individuals address what are defined as unique problems. Formal standards of conduct, procedures for seeking redress, and explicit penalties for people who violate prohibitions, all of which are fundamental components of legalistic social control (see Baumgartner, 1984:334–335), presuppose a specialized hierarchy to enforce them and are instead most compatible with the bureaucratic enterprise and other more hierarchical settings.

The unionized firm is one setting where legalistic social control appears with some regularity (Gersuny, 1973). Union contracts formalize the employment relationship in numerous ways, and normally include rules prohibiting certain conduct and describing precisely how employees can pursue grievances. The grievance process, which emulates a legal system, requires complainants to follow a series of steps when filing complaints. Aggrieved parties are provided union counsel to represent them, while formal hearings, complete with arbitrators, may be held to settle intractable disputes (Gersuny, 1973). Law-like systems of social control are also present in some nonunionized firms (Westin and Feliu, 1988). Several American companies, for example, have established independent judiciaries to handle workplace conflict and have granted rights of due process for employees (Ewing, 1989).

Contrary to the thesis that legalistic social control is associated with workplace democracy, formal grievance systems are found mainly in bureaucratic organizations. Unionization, for instance, is most prevalent in large manufacturing firms with traditional hierarchies. Moreover, there is a direct relationship between the number of employees in an organization, a rough measure of bureaucracy, and the likelihood it has nonunion grievance procedures (Scott, 1965; Edelman, 1990).[1] Smaller decentralized organizations, however, have few rules of any kind. For example, "[i]n comparison with bureaucratic organizations such as a government agency or corporation, [worker] collectives are characterized by the minimal use of formal, written rules" (Rothschild and Whitt, 1986:53). On communes, "each individual case is treated as unique. What is good for the community and what is good for the individual will be considered, never merely what legalism requires" (Zablocki, 1971: 231). And "legalism," including "explicit rights and duties," is generally not characteristic of the Japanese corporation (Rohlen, 1974:118).

Legalism is likewise rare at HelpCo. A formal code of conduct describes specific sanctions associated with several types of prohibited behavior. Yet, as noted in an earlier chapter, it is used only on occasion and restricted to parts of the firm where hierarchy is more developed than elsewhere. In the professional ranks, where authority is the most decentralized, the code of conduct is ignored.

Many social scientists are perplexed that democratically structured enterprises have not developed law-like systems of social control. One questions why "[s]ome of the safeguards that evolved in the societal arena to protect the individual from unjust authority are still absent from democratized firms" (Bernstein, 1982:68–69). But the absence of legalistic "safeguards" is not surprising. As Blackian theory predicts, people who are equal do not rely on rules to guide their interactions (Black, 1989:92, 1995:153).[2] Rules are created and enforced by authoritative third parties, who emerge only under conditions of inequality. In decentralized settings, the social control process, and social life more generally, is informal. Particularism rather than universalism is a guiding principle. Therapy, which in its pure form relies on informality and compromise, is therefore a natural byproduct of organizational democracy.[3]

## Therapeutic Communalism

Democracy alone does not produce therapy. Parties must be more than equal: They must be homogeneous and intimate. As shown in earlier chapters, therapy prospers in the postbureaucratic organization and other communal settings populated by people who are culturally similar and relationally close. Communalism creates an environment where behavior associated with therapy—observing others, delving into personal lives, communicating feelings, and so on—occurs in the normal course of events. It is likewise an environment where much of the self is public.

The communal character of social life at HelpCo is readily apparent. Individuals are keenly aware of coworkers' activities both on and off the job, a condition that some people find uncomfortable. One employee described the "pressure" associated with having so much of himself "exposed." Another claimed that working at HelpCo is like "living in a fish bowl." Similar experiences are reported by members of worker collectives: "[T]he small size and egalitarian nature of these groups and the close, personal relationships that knit them together, while adding satisfaction, also ironically contribute to stress" (Rothschild and Whitt, 1986:158).[4] On the Israeli kibbutz, "activities are reported and conversations are repeated, so that secrecy is all but impossible" (Spiro, 1956:99). According to one kibbutz member: "Everyone is concerned about public opinion. Here you can't escape it. Everyone in the kibbutz knows about everyone else. Sometimes it is too much so" (Spiro, 1956:99). Much of the self is also public on spiritual communes: "People do not work as if they had somebody watching them. Yet coexisting with all of this, is the consciousness that one's actions, and even one's thoughts, are somehow public" (Zablocki, 1971:227).[5]

As the postbureaucratic organization expands, the corporate world overall may become more communal, with privacy difficult and personal and professional lives meshed. Bendix anticipated a shift toward workplace communalism when he noted that the modern corporation increasingly regulates "not only our working hours but invades our homes and dictates our thoughts and dreams" (1956:339). Edwards (1979) arrived at a similar conclusion after reviewing the evolution of twentieth-century American business. He discovered that in the new capitalist enterprise, "workers owe not only a hard day's work, but also their demeanor and affections" (Edwards, 1979:148). In other words: "Hard work and deference are no longer enough; the 'soulful' corporation demands the worker's soul, or at least the worker's identity" (Edwards, 1979:151). In his recent study of a high-technology firm with a decentralized organizational structure and strong corporate culture, Kunda reports that employees experience "intense pressure, an invasion of their private life by corporate requirements, and in many cases, considerable personal suffering" (1992:223). Similarly, Barker (1993) found that the introduction of self-management teams at a small manufacturing company led to increased anxiety among workers. Team members, he discovered, monitor each other much more closely than superiors did under the old bureaucratic system. Consequently, individuals report that "peer pressure" can be intense (Barker, 1993:435).

Oddly enough, this modern communal setting has much in common with some of the earliest human societies. In many traditional settings, for example, people spend their entire lives among kinsmen and tribesmen whose cultural practices are identical and whose selves are largely public entities. Yet differences exist. The modern organizational "tribe" is more fluid and less encompassing. Membership is voluntary, and people have pasts and lives outside the organization. Communalism is thus strong, but impermanent and partial (see Black, 1976: 137).

The patterns of therapy in the postbureaucratic organization partly mirror those found in communal settings of the past. Even so, the temporary and fragmented nature of the modern communalism produces disparities as well. As Horwitz demonstrates, therapy is active in many tribal societies,[6] and like therapy elsewhere, including the postbureaucratic organization, "patients" frequently initiate and actively participate in the therapeutic process. But therapy in tribal societies is somewhat authoritative, resembling therapy in totalitarian societies such as the former Soviet Union and the People's Republic of China (1984:228–231). It is ritualistic, varying little across cases, and collective, involving relatives and other members of the community who encourage individuals to conform to demands of the group (228). Therapy in the postbureaucratic organization, by contrast, is informal and individualistic, more like modern psychiatry than therapy in other communal settings. Blackian theory explains this variation: The partial and fluid character of modern communal life means that the collective itself is less likely to exist as an entity superior to members as it is in tribal and totalitarian societies. And without superior third parties, authoritative social control, including authoritative therapy, cannot develop.

## Therapeutic Evolution

Therapy is increasingly found not only in corporations but in families, schools, and other formal and informal organizations. In the United States, for example, trained specialists offer a wide range of therapeutic services for people experiencing alleged mental problems. These specialists, who number more than one-half million, include professionals such as family therapists, social workers, clinical psychologists, and psychiatrists and "paraprofessionals" such as alcohol and drug abuse counselors. Thousands of therapeutic support groups, run by nonprofessionals, have also emerged in recent years to help individuals address problems of various kinds. "Self-help" books, instructing people how to cope with intrapersonal conflict on their own, are also popular, regularly appearing on bestseller lists.[7]

The government also provides and promotes therapy. Modern welfare states, for example, have elaborate bureaucracies run by professionals who have the authority to intervene in the mental lives of citizens. In America, "human service" agencies at the federal, state, and local level, including child welfare departments, vocational rehabilitation centers, homeless shelters, public assistance departments, and drug rehabilitation centers, identify and attempt to treat people thought to be experiencing mental difficulties (Polsky, 1991). The government also encourages, and sometimes demands, private groups to provide therapy for its members. For instance, many American corporations are required by law to make accommodations (and under some circumstances offer therapeutic services) to employees officially diagnosed as mentally ill (Olson, 1997). With the range of behavior classified as mental illness rapidly expanding (Davis, 1997), some companies hire attorneys whose sole responsibility is assuring compliance with the numerous mental health employment laws (Olson, 1997). As Blackian theory predicts, therapy sponsored by the state is more authoritative than when provided voluntarily by private individuals. People often have little choice but to comply with demands of state-sponsored therapists. Nonetheless, the superiority of the state is declining, especially in democratic societies. The most authoritarian forms of therapy are therefore rare. Asylums, for example, are disappearing, and lobotomies and electric-shock treatment are now considered barbaric by most modern governments.

Although authoritative and partisan social control, including violence, remain active under conditions of inequality and social distance, social space in organizations and elsewhere has been shrinking over the centuries (Black, 1993:155). Moralism therefore is "softening" and, as Black claims, "the population of enemies is declining" (1993:155). With the social conditions conducive to therapy on the rise, we might say that whereas enemies are vanishing the population of patients is increasing. But therapy does not eliminate enemies. It defines people as having conflicts with themselves. The enemy becomes the self.

Centralized authority is often considered a necessary condition for social order. Philosopher Thomas Hobbes, for example, claimed that without a strong sovereign state life would become "a war of everyone against everyone" (Hobbes, 1651:100). This book suggests that, at the organizational level at least, the absence of bureaucratic authority does not lead to interpersonal strife. Instead, therapy emerges. Rather than at war with everyone else, people are at war with themselves, or at least are regarded as such by others.

# Notes

1. Social control is "any process by which people define and respond to deviant behavior" (Black, 1984:21, n. 1). In other words, it is the handling of conflict, occurring whenever there is a "clash of right and wrong" (Black, 1998:xiii).

2. Authoritativeness and partisanship are the two variable aspects of third-party intervention identified by Black (1993: ch.7–8; 1995:834–837). The features of each and the social conditions that produce them are discussed later in this chapter.

3. Conflicts with the self might also be traced to supernatural forces (Black and Baumgartner, 1983:110; Black, 1984:12–13, n. 18; Horwitz, 1984:224).

4. Black first uses the term *pure sociology* in "A strategy of pure sociology" (1979). The features of his paradigm and its advantages are most thoroughly and forcefully presented in "The epistemology of pure sociology" (Black, 1995).

5. Black (1995:852–858) also introduces the concept of *social geometry* to refer to the location and direction of conflict (or other form of social life) in social space.

6. In the Blackian paradigm, *intimacy*, or relational distance, is a social rather than a psychological variable. It refers to the degree to "which people participate in each other's lives" (Black, 1976:40). It is measured by "the scope, frequency, and length of interaction between people, the age of their relationship, and the nature and number of links between them in a social network" (Black, 1976:41).

7. Social scientists often assume that sociological explanations must be causal, reducible to motivations or interests. Consequently, they may have difficulty understanding the distinctiveness of Black's theoretical strategy (see, e.g., Greenberg, 1983; Hunt, 1983). Blackian theory is not causal. Instead, it adopts a "covering-law" model of explanation (see, e.g., Braithwaite, 1953; Hempel, 1965; Homans, 1967:ch. 1). Behavior is explained when it is successfully deduced from a more general, higher-order statement (Black, 1979:150; see also Horwitz, 1983; Cooney, 1986:265).

8. The participants may be persons, groups, communities, and even societies (Black, 1995:837).

9. As Black notes, "The pattern I formulate is actually curvilinear, with law decreasing at the smallest and greatest distances in relational space, such as within families or friendships and between different societies and tribes. Within a single society such as modern America, however, the relationship is direct" (1995:832, n. 15).

10. Black identifies four styles of social control: penal, compensatory, conciliatory, and therapeutic (1976:4–6, 1884:8–12). *Penal* and *compensatory* social control are accusatory, meaning they determine winners and losers. The penal style subjects the guilty to pain, deprivation, or humiliation, whereas the compensatory style demands that the wrongdoer pays restitution to the injured party. *Conciliatory* and *therapeutic* social control are remedial, concerned with repairing relationships and individuals rather than blaming and condemning offenders. The conciliatory style aims to restore the relationship damaged by the conflict, whereas the therapeutic style is directed at the deviant party, who is treated as a victim in need of help.

11. Black introduces the phrase "the social structure of the case" in his book *Sociological Justice* (1989:8).

12. The scientific study of social control, apart from Black, has and continues to be mostly confined to law. Classical sociology, for example, was chiefly concerned with the formal mechanisms of social control initiated by the government. Emile Durkheim (1893) claimed that law reflects the nature of social solidarity. Marx and Engels understood law as an instrument of oppression, serving the interests of the wealthy at the expense of the poor (see Cain and Hunt, 1979). Max Weber (1925) traced the development of formal legal codes to the increasing rationality of modern Western societies.

Research on social control since these early statements also focuses mainly on law, but is more interested in documenting how disputes are actually handled than in developing theory about the relationship between law and society. The first wave of research focused on traditional settings, such as those explored by anthropologists. Llewellyn and Hoebel's (1941) study of conflict management among the Cheyenne Indians of North America was the first systematic investigation, and their focus on the handling of "trouble cases" inspired many other studies of law in small-scale societies. Several anthropologists directly observed the workings of courts in tribal Africa (e.g., Gluckman, 1955; Bohannan, 1957; Fallers, 1969). Others examined earlier stages of the disputing process among traditional people throughout the world (e.g., Gulliver, 1963; Nader and Metzger, 1963; Nader, 1965, Koch, 1974; Rothlenberger, 1978; Parnell, 1978; Starr, 1978; Todd, 1978).

Empirical studies of social control in modern settings are also preoccupied with law, and the American criminal justice system in particular. The police have received the most attention (e.g., Skolnick, 1966; Wilson, 1968; Black, 1970, 1971; Reiss, 1971; Manning, 1977), although research addresses the behavior of other legal officials as well (e.g., Sudnow, 1965; Mather, 1979; Gibson, 1980; Serron, 1988; Ynvegsson, 1988). Criminal sentencing has also been studied extensively (e.g., Chiricos and Waldo, 1975; Clarke and Koch, 1977; Lundsgaarde, 1977; Bowers and Pierce, 1980; Daly, 1987; Smith, 1987). Finally, research has explored, to a lesser extent, the handling of civil and regulatory cases of various kinds (e.g., Mayhew, 1968; Wanner, 1975, 1976; Yngvensson and Hennessey, 1975; Trubek, et al., 1983; Engel, 1984; Silberman, 1985).

13. In *The Social Structure of Right and Wrong*, Black (1993: ch. 8) also introduces a theory of *moralism*, authoritative behavior that includes violence initiated by third parties (including the state), superiors, equals, and subordinates. The book also contains a theory of *partisanship*, conduct that under some circumstances is collective violence (Black, 1993: Chapter 7).

14. This formulation is part of the Blackian explanation of therapy (see below).

15. As noted above, the handling of conflict is also referred to as *social control*. Students of the workplace, by contrast, frequently use the term "social control," or more often simply "control," in a different manner, to refer to mechanisms that employers use to motivate employees. (e.g., Etzioni, 1961; Simpson, 1985). Most have a normative orientation toward the subject matter. Management theorists, for example, tend to favor control strategies that contribute to the efficient functioning of organizations. Control is evaluated according to how well it succeeds in convincing employees to work toward the goals of employers (e.g., Tannenbaum, 1968; Simon, 1976). Labor market theorists, most who share neo-Marxian assumptions about the workplace, claim that control is an expression of capitalist domination. A primary concern is with showing how corporate authority prevents workers from pursuing their assumed collective interests (e.g., Edwards, 1979; Montgomery, 1980). Social scientists in the Weberian tradition consider control to be an impersonal force that can trap people in meaningless work environments (e.g. Biggart, 1989; Barker, 1993).

16. Szasz claims that "the metaphor of the self divided against itself is as central to psychiatry as the metaphor of the Trinity is to Christianity" (1994:107).

17. The party receiving therapy is usually a person, but it can also a group (Black, 1976:103, 1984:9 n. 13; compare Horwitz, 1990:94).

18. Horwitz (1984) finds that therapy is also somewhat authoritative in other settings, including tribal societies, where the community is elevated above the individual. He shows that

therapy of this kind—what he calls "communal therapy"—is found where group cohesion is high and individuals are subordinate to the community. "Individualistic therapy," Horwitz demonstrates, occurs under conditions of atomization, when people are free from the constraints of strong groups. It is nonauthoritative, focusing on the unique experiences of individuals and seeking to enhance autonomy.

19. These kinds of therapy are similar in some ways to what Black and Baumgartner (1983:106–107) call "repressive pacification," the most authoritative form of third-party intervention. The self is "cured" despite its wishes. Horwitz limits his use of therapy to persuasive efforts to control the self. He therefore calls coercive attempts to change personalities "indoctrination" rather than therapy (Horwitz, 1984:213–215).

20. The formulation also explains why self-intimacy increases self-therapy: The closer the principals (the self), the less likelihood of third-party intervention (therapy) (Black, 1995: 836 n. 37).

21. This includes self-intimacy.

22. On therapy in preindustrial societies, see, e.g., Gibbs, 1963; Kiev, 1964; Frank, 1973; Lambo, 1974.

23. Although mostly ignored by sociologists, the role of therapy in organizations has been a common object of study among clinicians. Research psychologists have generated a sizeable literature on the effectiveness of alcohol treatment and other mental health programs on employee behavior (see Kemp, 1994). Thus far, however, few attempts have been made to explain the presence of such programs, other than to claim they fulfill some kind of organizational function or psychological need (but see Roman, 1980). The clinical literature also ignores informal therapy, applied by employees themselves during the course of their everyday work lives.

24. The "postbureaucratic" organization (Bennis, 1966; Barker, 1993; Heckscher and Donnellon, 1994) is just one of the names given to enterprises that self-consciously reduce bureaucracy. Others include the "organic" system of management (Burns and Stalker, 1961), "Type Z" company (Ouchi, 1981), "postentrepreunerial" firm (Kanter, 1989), and "network" organizational form (Powell, 1990).

25. In a 1992 survey of almost 700 U.S. manufacturing establishments, Osterman (1994) found that over one-third made "substantial use of innovative work practices," including self-directed employee teams, job rotation, and quality circles. Based on a review of several national level surveys, Applebaum and Batt discovered that since 1982, "the proportion of firms with at least one employee-involvement practice somewhere in the company is large and growing" (1994:60). Two-thirds have at least one quality circle and about one-half have at least one self-directed team.

26. Ownership is most often in the form of an employee stock ownership plan (ESOP), an arrangement whereby employees gradually acquire shares of stock (Rosen, Klein, and Young, 1986). The ESOP is discussed in greater detail in chapter 2.

27. Employees own a majority of the stock in about one-fourth of the employee-owned corporations (Rosen, Klein, and Young, 1986).

28. The growing popularity of this form of organization has not gone unnoticed by social scientists. But most research on enterprises that limit bureaucracy addresses issues unrelated to conflict (but see Mansbridge, 1980:ch. 13). One kind of study is concerned with whether these organizations are more productive than conventional bureaucratic firms (e.g., Ouchi, 1981; Kanter, 1983, 1989). Another critically examines the ability of these enterprises to live up to certain democratic standards (e.g., Toscano, 1983; Russell, 1985).

29. Corporate managers and other professionals, for example, sometimes work in settings where informality and interpersonal trust are more important than the specialized hierarchy (Dalton, 1959; Burns and Stalker, 1961; Friedson, 1975; Kanter, 1977). Also, lower-level members of bureaucracies, because of their unique skills or access to privileged knowledge, frequently have more authority than the prescribed organizational structure suggests. The demands of organizational life may reduce social distance between subordinates and superiors as well (Whyte, 1948; Roy, 1952; Gouldner, 1953, 1954; Scheff, 1961; Mechanic, 1962; Kanter, 1977). Under these conditions, therapy would be expected to emerge.

30. Therapy in the workplace is also not an entirely new phenomenon. Earlier this century, for instance, organizational reformers promoted a "human relations" approach to management (Mayo, 1933; Roethlisberger and Dickson, 1939). Inappropriate conduct was traced to psychological factors, including those thought to be caused by the work environment itself, rather than the inherent inadequacy of individual employees. Abandoning the prevailing view that employees were motivated solely by material considerations, reformers encouraged companies to address so-called emotional and social needs. Few organizations immediately embraced the humanistic approach, but its appearance may have reflected (and can be explained by) the beginning of a shift away from the traditional bureaucratic structure.

## Chapter Two

1. Many classic studies of the workplace are of single enterprises: Gouldner (1954), for example, conducted research at a mining company, Dalton (1959) at a manufacturing firm, and Kanter (1977) at an industrial supply corporation. Recent studies include, among many others, Martin's (1992) and Kunda's (1992) research on enterprises in the high-technology industry, V. Smith's (1990) ethnography of a large bank, and Paules' (1991) investigation as a participant-observer of a small restaurant.

2. Each year the firm donates shares from an ownership trust (containing shares purchased from the founder, who prior to 1975 owned all the corporate stock) to employees with over one year of service. Individuals are entitled to a portion of their shares after four years on the job, at which point they are, in company language, 40 percent "vested" (they own 40 percent of their stock). The "vesting" rate increases 20 percent each subsequent year, meaning that after seven years at HelpCo employees are entitled to all the stock allocated to their accounts. When employees leave the firm, they can either keep their allocated shares or sell them back to the company. More than 50 percent of the stock has been allocated from the trust to nonexecutive employees and 10 percent to executives (president and

department directors). Less than 5 percent is held by former employees. The balance remains in the trust to be allocated in the future. Like all employee stock ownership plans (ESOPs), the amount of stock allocated to an employee account is partially based on salary. As a result, supervisors and directors receive more shares. Yet because the pay differentials are not as dramatic as in traditional firms—the highest paid executive earns about six times as much as the lowest paid hourly worker—the differences in share ownership are not as significant as they are in other ESOP companies.

3. Research shows that employee ownership does not necessarily lead to greater worker participation in company affairs (Rosen, Klein, and Young, 1986).

4. The decentralized structure of social relations presented a challenge in recruiting interviewees. In bureaucratic settings, enlisting subjects through the hierarchy is possible. Supervisors simply instruct subordinates to participate. At HelpCo, employees had to be persuaded to take part in the project. The process of recruiting participants was coordinated by the department directors. I asked each director to encourage a cross section of ten to fifteen individuals in their departments to volunteer. After describing the study to employees in meetings and memorandum, the directors met this request. The final sample included a slightly disproportionate number of supervisors and long-term employees in comparison to those in lower-level positions and newer employees. This is not necessarily a drawback. In this type of study, a higher percentage of supervisors and long-term employees are preferred, since they are likely to have the most experience with social control.

5. I recorded thirty-two of the interviews and later transcribed the tapes.

6. The formal interviews followed a schedule with fifty open-ended questions. On the first series of questions I obtained details about the interviewee's job and relationship with other employees. The second and most extensive set addressed how individuals at HelpCo typically pursue differences with other employees. I was particularly concerned with gathering specific instances of social control in which the interviewee had been a participant or observer. For each of these cases, employees were asked to comment on the source of the problem, initial reac-

tions, the extent to which parties other than the principals were involved, the length of the disagreement, and the resolution, if any. The informal interviews relied less on specific questions on the interview guide. Since many of these interviews were done over lunch at local restaurants or with more than one employee present, I was constrained to address the issues in a more casual manner.

7. The one exception was a production employee who had been with the firm less than a year. She was very uneasy during the interview, and was unwilling to elaborate much on her experiences. Only two employees mentioned the tape recorder while being interviewed. In the first instance it was done in a humorous context. After registering his dislike for a new product idea sponsored by several executives, a team leader remarked: "I don't know if you want my opinion of that idea on your tape recorder." He then laughed and went on to express his opinion. The other employee, a marketing research employee, understandably wanted assurance that information on the tape would be kept confidential.

8. I also relied on my ethnographic presence to discern the predominant patterns of social control. Although it was impossible to quantify the material in any meaningful way, I developed a rough coding scheme to summarize the cases. I first classified cases by their direction, whether downward, lateral, or upward (on the direction of social control, see Black 1976). Downward cases (93 of the 252 cases) are those in which social control flows from superiors to subordinates. Lateral cases (88) occur between peers, and upward cases (71) are those in which subordinates direct social control toward superiors. For each case, I noted all of the efforts taken by the offended party to resolve the problem. In some cases, individuals simply complained to a coworker and let the case drop. In others, they responded in several ways, such as talking to the offender, seeking assistance from a manager, modifying their own behavior, and attempting to implement an organizational level change. Some cases overlapped so that identifying the start of one case and the end of another was difficult. The data are therefore such that providing frequencies and cross-tabulations of social control cases would be cumbersome and ultimately not very useful.

## Chapter Three

1. More specifically, Black proposes that discipline is most severe in a "parasitical hierarchy," a "social field" that includes the following characteristics: inequality, vertical segmentation, social distance, functional unity, and immobility (1990:47–49).

2. Inequality refers mainly to differences in vertical status (wealth), but can also refer to differences in integration, conventionality, and respectability (Black, 1995:836 n. 38). Difference in the level of organization is also a kind of inequality. Social distance includes both relational and cultural distance (see Black, 1989:176; 1990:46).

3. Written warnings are in fact themselves threats, but of a more formal nature. They indicate that a supervisor is unsatisfied with the performance of a subordinate and that if his or her conduct does not change, harsher sanctions are in order.

4. As discussed in chapter 5, this method of termination reflects a concern with possible legal retaliation by dismissed employees.

5. Morrill found that informal counseling is a conflict management strategy occasionally used by executives in bureaucratic corporations (1995:107–110).

6. The frequent use of higher-ranking male allies among females may be related to their unique structural position. Women supervisors tend to be lower in rank and seniority than their male counterparts. Females are therefore at a relative disadvantage when initiating social control. This liability is most significant when offending subordinates are male. Bringing in a male ally increases the stature of the female supervisor and weakens the effect of any gender difference. As others have noted, successful businesswomen are likely to have male mentors to help them fight gender stereotypes and climb the corporate hierarchy (Kanter, 1977:181–184; Morrill, 1995:85–87). Most females who have made it into the management ranks have ready access to male allies.

7. Hugh has several books in his office that describe this psychotherapeutic technique. He also has the latest issues of *Transactional Analysis Journal*.

8. Social psychologists might interpret Peggy's behavior dif-

ferently. Kanter, for example, traces the domineering behavior of female managers to their scarcity in low-level management positions (1977:201–205). Because women are in leadership positions with little real authority, they compensate for their lack of power by acting "mean and bossy" and exerting what limited authority they do have.

## Chapter Four

1. Peers are those who are not linked vertically in a formal hierarchy. They may differ in rank (determined by wage or salary), for example, or respectability (Morrill, 1989:403–405, 1995: ch. 6).

2. The social field associated with severe vengeance is a "stable agglomeration," characterized by equality, social distance, immobility, functional independence, and organization (Black, 1990:44–47).

3. Even so, the capriciousness of vengeance varies. Feuding, for example, is a kind of vengeance and in its classic form "is an even exchange of killings over a period of time, each side keeping score and openly repricating each loss it suffers" (Black, 1995:855 n. 130). Black introduces a model of feuding and theorizes that it occurs in settings where highly intimate and homogeneous groups are equal and culturally similar to each other, relationally segmented and functionally independent, and separated by an intermediate level of relational distance: "Narrow the distances in the model by reducing the relational separation and independence of the parties, and the reciprocity and continuity of the violence declines. Increase the distances, including the relational and cultural distances, and the violence becomes more indiscriminate and warlike" (Black, 1995:855 n. 130).

4. Black calls the social field conducive to authoritative settlement a "triangular hierarchy." It includes these variables: inequality, relational distance, isosceles triangulation, heterogeneity, organizational asymmetry (Black, 1990:56–58).

5. Not all physicians handle their disputes in this manner. For example, in a hospital outside Boston, an anesthesiologist and a surgeon were recently fined $10,000 for wrestling on the

floor of an operating room while a patient was under general anesthesia. Besides the fine, the state board of medicine put both doctors on five years probation and ordered them to undergo joint psychotherapy (*The New York Times*, November 28, 1993).

6. Silbey and Merry (1986) identify "therapeutic mediation" as a type of professional mediation strategy that centers on the personalities of the adversaries.

7. Marxian scholars, who often criticize organizational theorists for representing the interests of owners and managers, are usually normative and psychological in their analysis of capitalist organizations. Capitalism is thought to produce "alienation" and "false consciousness," largely psychological conditions that can only be overcome by giving workers ownership and control over the means of production. Marxism thus has a therapeutic dimension. In fact, Szasz calls Karl Marx a "social therapist" (1961:54).

## Chapter Five

1. Black theorizes that rebellion, like discipline, is most severe in a "parasitical hierarchy," a social field characterized by inequality, vertical segmentation, social distance, functional unity, and immobility (1990:47–49).

2. This finding conforms to a more general pattern: People everywhere tend not to submit their conflicts for settlement to those of lower rank (Black and Baumgartner, 1983:113; Baumgartner, 1988:68). Apparently, the same pattern applies to intrapersonal conflict.

3. Senechal de la Roche, applying Blackian theory, shows how collective violence is a direct function of "social polarization," including relational and cultural distance, inequality, and functional independence. The last variable is applied to workplace conflict: "Variation in the degree of functional independence between workers and employers . . . helps explain patterns of collective violence in industrial societies" (Senechal de la Roche, 1996:112).

4. Baumgartner shows how dependent wives may turn to male relatives for help in handling domestic conflict (1984:318–319).

5. In the mid-1980s, several employees met with a regional union in an attempt to organize the hourly workers. A union official tried to rally support and eventually administered a vote, but employees soundly defeated the effort.

6. A lawsuit is technically an authoritative form of third-party settlement rather than unilateral rebellion. Moreover, lawsuits are compensatory rather than penal because they seek to give plaintiffs financial restitution for alleged suffering. Yet defendants can be subject to punitive damages as well. Moreover, the threat of a suit itself is punitive and might therefore be classified as a kind of rebellion.

On the increasing tendency of individuals to hold organizations liable for their misfortunes, see Black (1987).

7. Jenny did mention the possibility that another employee may have been the "phantom pisser." If so, the actual offender may have quit urinating on the floor after Dennis resigned, realizing he would be blamed for the conduct.

8. Consequently, these behaviors are better classified as downward therapy rather than upward therapy. Subordinates are seeking help from above by displaying distress (see Baumgartner, 1984:324–331).

9. "Theory X" refers to a management philosophy that assumes individuals naturally dislike work and therefore need to be tightly supervised. "Theory Y," in contrast, assumes people enjoy work and will be productive if they are given autonomy (McGregor, 1960). "Theory Z" is a term used by Ouchi (1981) to describe the decentralized, collaborative style of management found in Japanese corporations.

10. The actual name of the system used by HelpCo has been disguised.

11. Though more formal than most social control at HelpCo, *Open Up* differs from grievance systems found in other organizations, where prescribed procedures allow employees to take action only when specified rules have been violated by superiors. With *Open Up,* any grievance is considered legitimate. The anonymous option allows employees to criticize others without, in the words of one manager, "hurting their feelings."

12. The appearance of this type of complaint is probably related to the fact that employees own the firm and are therefore

more concerned about holding down costs than employees in traditional capitalist firms.

## Chapter Six

1. Most research on legalistic governance and social control policies simply examines their presence in organizations. The extent to which they are used is rarely addressed (but see Gersuny, 1973).

2. The theory of law developed by Black (1976) also anticipates an inverse relationship between organizational democracy and legalistic social control. As Black shows, law (governmental social control) is least developed in settings with minimal hierarchy and centralization of authority (1976:ch. 2, 5; see also Black, 1989:ch. 6).

3. Mansbridge (1980) identifies two kinds of democracies: *unitary* and *adversary*. Unitary democracies tend to be small groups, with members arriving at consensual decisions through face-to-face interaction. Adversary democracies are typically larger bodies, including nation states, where elected officials, often with competing interests, debate issues in formal legislative arenas. It may be that the direct relationship between therapy and democracy does not apply to adversary democracies, which by their nature have more hierarchy and social distance. In fact, legalism appears to be a fundamental part of adversary democracies.

4. Some accounts of life in small-scale decentralized organizations show that group pressure can lead to various physical reactions. Mansbridge, for example, discovered that members in worker collectives suffer a disproportionate number of headaches due to the pressure of having to work with close friends and live up to their expectations (1980:126).

5. Zablocki calls the Bruderhof commune a "totalitarian society" (1971:193).

6. Horwitz (1984) mainly addresses variation in what he calls the styles of therapy—communal and individualistic—rather the quantity of therapy (but see Horwitz, 1990:81–86, 90–95). Blackian theory, however, predicts that remedial social

control, including therapy, is attracted to tribal settings with high levels of homogeneity and intimacy.

7. Information on the growth of therapeutic services in modern America comes from Horwitz (1990:246–247) and Rice (1996:27–28, 48–52).

# References

Adizes, Ichak
  1971   *Industrial Democracy: Yugoslav Style.* New York: Free
         Press.
Ashton, T. S.
  1955   *An Economic History of England: The 18th Century.*
         London: Methuen and Company.
Appelbaum, Eileen, and Rosemary Batt
  1994   *The New American Workplace: Transforming Work
         Systems in the United States.* Ithaca: ILR Press.
Balzer, Richard
  1976   *Clockwork: Life in and Outside an American Factory.*
         Garden City, New York: Doubleday and Company.
Barker, James R.
  1993   "Tightening the Iron Cage: concertive control in self-
         managing teams." *Administrative Science Quarterly*
         38:408–437.
Bartunek, Jean M., and Robin D. Reid
  1992   "The role of conflict in a second order change at-
         tempt." Pages 116–142 in *Hidden Conflict in Organi-*

zations: Uncovering Behind-the-Scenes Disputes, edited by Deborah M. Kolb and Jean M. Bartunek. Newbury Park: Sage.

Baumgartner, M. P.

1978    Law and social status in colonial New Haven." Pages 153–178 in Research in Law and Sociology: An Annual Compilation of Research, Volume 1, edited by Rita J. Simon. Greenwich: JAI Press.

1984    "Social control from below." Pages 303–345 in Toward a General Theory of Social Control, Volume 1: Fundamentals, edited by Donald Black. Orlando: Academic Press.

1988    The Moral Order of a Suburb. New York: Oxford University Press.

1992    "War and peace in early childhood." Pages 1–38 in Virginia Review of Sociology, Volume 1: Law and Conflict Management, edited by James Tucker. Greenwich: JAI Press.

Bendix, Reinhard

1956    Work and Authority in Industry: Ideologies of Management in the Course of Industrialization. New York: Harper and Row.

Bennis, Warren

1966    Changing Organizations. New York: McGraw-Hill.

Bernstein, Paul

1982    "Necessary elements for effective worker-participation in decision-making." Pages 51–81 in Workplace Democracy and Social Change, edited by Frank Lindenfeld and Joyce Rothschild-Whitt. Boston: Porter Sargent Publishers.

Biggart, Nichole Woosley

1989    Charismatic Capitalism: Direct Selling Organizations in America. Chicago: University of Chicago Press.

Black, Donald

1970    "Production of crime rates." American Sociological Review 35:733–748.

1971    "The social organization of arrest." Stanford Law Review. 23:1087–1111.

1976    The Behavior of Law. New York: Academic Press.

1979    "A strategy of pure sociology." Pages 149–168 in *The-oretical Perspectives in Sociology*, edited by Scott G. McNall. New York: St. Martin's Press.

1980    "A note on the measurement of law." Pages 209–217 in *The Manners and Customs of the Police*: New York: Academic Press.

1983    "Crime as social control." *American Sociological Review* 48:34–45.

1984    "Social control as a dependent variable." Pages 1–35 in *Toward a General Theory of Social Control*, Volume 1: *Fundamentals*, edited by Donald Black. Orlando: Academic Press.

1987    "Compensation and the social structure of misfortune." *Law and Society Review* 21:563–584.

1989    *Sociological Justice*. New York: Oxford University Press.

1990    "The elementary forms of conflict management." Pages 43–69 in *New Directions in the Study of Justice, Law, and Social Control*, prepared by the School of Justice Studies, Arizona State University. New York: Plenum Press.

1992    "Social control of the self." Pages 39–50 in *Virginia Review of Sociology*, Volume 1: *Law and Conflict Management*, edited by James Tucker. Greenwich: JAI Press.

1993    *The Social Structure of Right and Wrong*. San Diego: Academic Press.

1995    "The epistemology of pure sociology." *Law and Social Inquiry* 20:829–870.

1998    "Prologue to the Revised Edition." Pages xiii–xxii in *The Social Structure of Right and Wrong*. San Diego: Academic Press (revised edition).

Black, Donald, and M. P. Baumgartner
1983    "Toward a theory of the third-party." Pages 84–114 in *Empirical Theories about Courts*, edited by Keith O. Boyum and Lynn Mather. New York: Longman.

Bohannan, Paul
1957    *Justice and Judgement among the Tiv*. London: Oxford University Press.

Borg, Marian J.
1992    "Conflict management in the world system." *Socio-logical Forum* 7:261–282.

Bowers, William J., and Glenn L Pierce
1980    "Arbitrariness and discrimination under post-*Furman* capital statues." *Crime and Delinquency* 26:563–635.

Braithwaite, Richard Bevan
1953    *Scientific Explanation: A Study of the Function of Theory, Probability and Law in Science.* New York: Harper and Row.

Brecher, Jeremy
1972    *Strike!* San Francisco: Straight Arrow Books.

Burns, Tom, and George MacPherson Stalker
1961    *The Management of Innovation.* New York: Barnes and Noble.

Cain, Maureen, and Alan Hunt (editors)
1979    *Marx and Engels on Law.* London: Academic Press.

Chiricos, Theodore G., and Gordon P. Waldo
1975    "Socioeconomic status and criminal sentencing: an empirical assessment of a conflict proposition." *American Sociological Review* 40:753–772.

Clarke, Steven H., and Gary G. Koch
1977    "The influence of income and other factors on whether criminal defendants go to prison." *Law and Society Review* 11:57–92.

Collinson, David L.
1992    *Managing the Shopfloor: Subjectivity, Masculinity and Workplace Culture.* Berlin: Walter de Gruyter.

Conrad, Peter, and Joseph W. Schneider
1980    *Deviance and Medicalization: From Badness to Sickness.* St. Louis: C. V. Mosby.

Cooney, Mark
1986    "Behavioural sociology of law: a defence." *Modern Law Review* 49:262–271.

1988    The Social Control of Homicide: A Cross-Cultural Study. Unpublished Doctoral Dissertation, Harvard Law School.

1991    Law, Morality, and Conscience: The Social Control of Homicide in Modern America. Unpublished Doctoral

Dissertation, Department of Sociology, University of Virginia.

1998    *Warriors and Peacemakers: How Third Parties Shape Violence.* New York: New York University Press.

Dalton, Dan R., and Debra J. Mesch

1990    "The impact of flexible scheduling on employee attendance and turnover." *Administrative Science Quarterly* 35:370–387.

Dalton, Melvin

1959    *Men Who Manage Fusions of Feeling and Theory in Administration.* New York: Wiley.

Daly, Kathleen

1987    "Discrimination in the criminal court: family, gender, and the problem of equal treatment." *Social Forces* 66: 152–175.

Davis, L. J.

1997    "The encyclopedia of insanity: a psychiatric handbook lists a madness for everyone." *Harper's Magazine* Febuary:61–66.

Dean, Warren

1976    *Rio Carlo: A Brazilian Plantation System, 1820–1920.* Stanford: Stanford University Press.

Dinitz, Simon, Mark Lefton, Shirley Angrist, and Benjamin Pasamanik

1961    "Psychiatric and social attributes as predictors of case outcome in mental hospitalization." *Social Problems* 8(Spring):322–328.

Durkheim, Emile

1893    *The Division of Labor in Society.* New York: Free Press, 1964.

Edelman, Lauren B.

1990    "Legal environments and organizational governance: the expansion of due process in the American workplace." *American Journal of Sociology* 95:1401–1440.

Edwards, Richard

1979    *Contested Terrain: The Transformation of the Workplace in the Twentieth Century.* New York: Basic Books.

Engel, David M.
1984    "The oven bird's song: insiders, outsiders, and personal injuries in an American community." *Law and Society Review* 18:551–582.

Etzioni, Amatai
1961    *A Comparative Analysis of Complex Organizations.* New York: Free Press.

Ewing, David
1989    *Justice on the Job: Resolving Grievances in the Nonunion Workplace.* Boston: Harvard Business School Press.

Fain, Scott T.
1980    "Self-employed Americans: their number has increased." *Monthly Labor Review.* 103:3–8

Fallers, Lloyd A.
1969    *Law without Precedent: Legal Ideas in Action in the Courts of Colonial Busoga.* Chicago: University of Chicago Press.

Fireside, Harvey
1979    *Soviet Psychoprisons.* New York: W. W. Norton and Company.

Frank, Jerome D.
1973    *Persuasion and Healing.* Baltimore: John Hopkins University Press (second edition).

Friedman, Raymond A.
1992    "The culture of mediation: private understandings in the context of public conflict." Pages 143–164 in *Hidden Conflict in Organizations: Uncovering Behind-the-Scenes Disputes*, edited by Deborah M. Kolb and Jean M. Bartunek. Newbury Park: Sage.

Friedson, Eliot
1975    *Doctoring Together: A Study of Professional Social Control.* Chicago: University of Chicago Press.

Garrison, Vivian
1977    "Doctor, espiritista, or psychiatrists? health seeking behavior in a Puerto Rico neighborhood of New York City." *Medical Anthropology* 1 (entire issue).

Gartman, David
1986    *Auto Slavery: The Labor Process in the American Au-*

*tomobile Industry, 1857–1950.* New Brunswick, New Jersey: Rutgers University Press.

Gersuny, Carl
1973    *Punishment and Redress in a Modern Factory.* Lexington: Lexington Books.

Gibbs, James L., Jr.
1963    "The Kpelle moot: a therapeutic model for the informal settlement of disputes." *Africa* 33:1–10.

Gibson, James
1980    "Environmental constraints on the behavior of judges: a representational model of judicial decision-making." *Law and Society Review* 14:343–370.

Glickman, Rose L.
1984    *Russian Factory Women: Workplace and Society, 1880–1914.* Berkeley: University of California Press.

Gluckman, Max
1955    *The Judicial Process among the Barotse of Northern Rhodesia.* Manchester: Manchester University Press.
1963    "Gossip and scandal." *Current Anthropology* 4:307–316.

Goffman, Erving
1961    *Asylums: Essays on the Social Situation of Mental Patients and Other Inmates.* Garden City: Anchor Books.

Gouldner, Alvin
1953    *Wildcat Strike.* New York: Free Press.
1954    *Patterns of Industrial Bureaucracy.* New York: Free Press.

Grabosky, Peter N.
1984    "The variability of punishment." Pages 163–189 in *Toward a General Theory of Social Control*, Volume 1: *Fundamentals*, edited by Donald Black. Orlando: Academic Press.

Greenberg, David F.
1983    "Donald Black's sociology of law: a critique." *Law and Society Review* 17:337–368.

Grob, Gerald N.
1973    *Mental Institutions in America: Social Policy to 1875.* New York: Free Press.

Gross, Jan T.
    1984    "Social control under totalitarianism." Pages 55–79 in
            *Toward a General Theory of Social Control*, Volume
            2: *Selected Problems*, edited by Donald Black. Or-
            lando: Academic Press.
Gulliver, Phillip H.
    1963    *Social Control in an African Society: A study of the
            Arusha, Agricultural Masai of Northern Tanganyika.*
            Boston: Boston University Press.
Gwartney-Gibbs, Patricia A., and Denise H. Lach
    1991    "Workplace dispute resolution and gender inequal-
            ity." *Negotiation Journal* 7,2:187–200.
Hammond, J. L., and Barbara Hammond
    1968    *The Town Labourer.* Garden City: Doubleday Anchor
            Books.
Heckscher, Charles, and Lynda M. Applegate
    1994    "Introduction." Pages 1–13 in *The Post-Bureaucratic
            Organization: New Perspectives on Organizational
            Change*, edited by Charles Heckscher and Anne Don-
            nellon. Thousand Oaks: Sage.
Heckscher, Charles, and Anne Donnellon (editors)
    1994    *The Post-Bureaucratic Organization: New Perspec-
            tives on Organizational Change.* Thousand Oaks:
            Sage.
Hempel, Carl G.
    1965    "Aspects of scientific explanation." Pages 331–496
            in *Aspects of Scientific Explanation and Other Es-
            says in the Philosophy of Science.* New York: Free
            Press.
Hermann, John
    1992    "Gossip in science." Paper presented at the 1992 an-
            nual meeting of the American Sociological Associa-
            tion.
Hershatter, Gail
    1986    *The Workers of Tianjin, 1900–1949.* Stanford: Stan-
            ford University Press.
Hobbes, Thomas
    1651    *Leviathan.* New York: Macmillian, 1962.
Hoch, Steven L.
    1986    *Serfdom and Social Control in Russia: Petrovskoe, a*

*Village in Tambov*. Chicago: University of Chicago Press.

Hodson, Randy
1991    "The active worker: compliance and autonomy in the workplace." *Journal of Contemporary Ethnography* 20,1:47–78.

Homans, George Casper
1967    *The Nature of Social Science*. New York: Harcourt, Brace, and World.

Horwitz, Allan V.
1982    *The Social Control of Mental Illness*. New York: Academic Press.

1983    "Resistance to innovation in the sociology of law: a response to Greenberg." *Law and Society Review* 17: 369–384.

1984    "Therapy and social solidarity." Pages 211–250 in *Toward a General Theory of Social Control*, Volume 1: *Fundamentals*, edited by Donald Black. Orlando: Academic Press.

1990    *The Logic of Social Control*. New York: Plenum Press.

Hunt, Alan
1983    "Behavioral sociology of law: a critique of Donald Black." *Journal of Law and Society* 10:19–46.

Jackall, Robert
1984    "A paradox of collective work: a study of the Cheeseboard, Berkeley, California. Pages 109–135 in *Worker Cooperatives in America*, edited by Robert Jackall and Henry M. Levin. Berkeley: University of California Press.

Jackall, Robert, and Henry M. Levin
1984    *Worker Cooperatives in America*. Berkeley: University of California Press.

Jermier, John M., David Knights, and Walter R. Nord (editors)
1994    *Resistance and Power in Organizations*. London: Routledge.

Kanter, Rosabeth Moss
1972    *Commitment and Community*. Cambridge: Cambridge University Press.

1977    *Men and Women of the Corporation*. New York: Basic Books.

1983   *Changemasters*. New York: Simon and Schuster.

1989   *When Giants Learn To Dance*. New York: Simon and Schuster.

Kemp, Donna R.

1994   *Mental Health in the Workplace: An Employer's and Manager's Guide*. Westport, Connecticut: Quorum Books.

Kephart, William M.

1976   *Extraordinary Groups: The Sociology of Unconventional Life-Styles*. New York: St. Martin's Press.

Kiev, Ari (editor)

1964   *Magic, Faith, and Healing: Studies in Primitive Psychiatry Today*. New York: Free Press.

Kincade, Kathleen

1973   *A Walden Two Experiment: The First Five Years of Twin Oaks Community*. New York: Morrow.

Koch, Klaus-Friedrich

1974   *War and Peace in Jalemo: The Management of Conflict in Highland New Guinea*. Cambridge: Harvard University Press.

Kolb, Deborah M., and Jean M Bartunek (editors)

1992   *Hidden Conflict in Organizations: Uncovering Behind-the-Scenes Disputes*. Newbury Park: Sage.

Kunda, Gideon

1992   *Engineering Culture: Control and Commitment in a High-Tech Corporation*. Philadelphia: Temple University Press.

Laing, R. D.

1960   *The Divided Self*. New York: Pantheon Books.

Lambo, Thomas Adeoye

1974   "Psychotherapy in Africa." *Psychotherapy and Psychosomatics* 24:311–326.

Lawler, Edward J.

1992   "Affective attachments to nested groups: a choice-process theory." *American Sociological Review* 57: 327–39.

Leland, Mrs. Wilfred C.

1966   *Master of Precision: Henry M. Leland*. Detroit: Wayne State University Press.

Lin, T., K. Tardiff, G. Donetz, and W. Goresky
1978  "Ethnicity and patterns of help seeking." *Culture, Medicine, and Psychiatry* 2:3–14.

Linsky, Arnold S.
1970  "Who shall be excluded: the influence of personal attributes in community reaction to the mentally ill." *Social Psychiatry* 5:166–171.

Llewellyn, Karl N., and E. Adamson Hoebel
1941  *The Cheyenne Way: Conflict and Case Law in Primitive Jurisprudence.* Norman: University of Oklahoma Press.

Lundsgaarde, Henry P.
1977  *Murder in Space City: A Cultural Analysis of Houston Homicide Patterns.* New York: Oxford University Press.

Manning, Peter
1977  *Police Work: The Social Organization of Policing.* Cambridge: M.I.T. Press.

Mansbridge, Jane J.
1980  *Beyond Adversary Democracy.* New York: Basic Books.

Martin, Joanne
1992  *Culture in Organizations: Three Perspectives.* New York: Oxford University Press.

Mather, Lynn
1979  *Plea Bargaining or Trial? The Process of Criminal Case Disposition.* Lexington: Lexington Press.

Mayhew, Leon
1968  *Law and Discrimination: A Study of the Massachusetts Commission Against Discrimination.* Cambridge: Harvard University Press.

Mayo, Elton
1933  *The Human Problems of Industrial Civilization.* New York: Macmillian.

McGregor, Douglas
1960  *The Human Side of Enterprise.* New York: McGraw-Hill.

Mechanic, David
1962  "Sources of power of lower participants in complex organizations." *Administrative Science Quarterly* 7: 349–364.

Merry, Sally Engle
1984  "Rethinking gossip and scandal." Pages 271–302 in
       *Toward a General Theory of Social Control*, Volume
       1: *Fundamentals*, edited by Donald Black. Orlando:
       Academic Press.

Montgomery, David
1980  *Workers' Control in America: Studies in History of
       Work, Technology, and Labor Struggles.* New York:
       Cambridge University Press.

Morrill, Calvin
1989  "The management of managers: disputing in an ex-
       ecutive hierarchy." *Sociological Forum* 4:387–407.

1992  "Vengeance among executives." Pages 51–76 in *Vir-
       ginia Review of Sociology*, Volume 1: *Law and Conflict
       Management*, edited by James Tucker. Greenwich: JAI
       Press.

1995  *The Executive Way: Conflict Management in Corpo-
       rations.* Chicago: University of Chicago Press.

Müller, Hans-Heinrich
1991  "Migrant workers from East-Elbe and Eastern Europe
       in the Prussian 'Sugerbeet' Province of Saxony, 1830–
       1914." Pages 77–91 in *Migrants in Agricultural De-
       velopment: A Study of Intrarural Migration*, edited
       J. A. Mollet. New York: New York University Press.

Mullis, Jeffrey
1995  "Medical malpractice, social structure, and social
       control." *Sociological Forum* 10:135–163.

Nader, Laura
1965  "Choices in legal procedure: Shia Moslem and Mex-
       ican Zapotec." *American Anthropologist* 67:394–
       399.

Nader, Laura, and Duane Metzger
1963  "Conflict resolution in two Mexican communities."
       *American Anthropologist* 65:584–592.

Nader, Laura, and Harry F. Todd
1978  *The Disputing Process: Law in Ten Societies.* New
       York: Columbia University Press.

Nevins, Alan
1954  *Ford: The Times, The Man, The Company.* New York:
       Scribner.

Olson, Walter K.
 1997    *The Excuse Factory: How Employment Law is Para-
         lyzing the American Workplace.* New York: Free
         Press.
Ong, Aihwa
 1987    *Spirits of Resistance and Capitalist Decline: Factory
         Women in Malaysia.* Albany: State University of New
         York Press.
Osterman, Paul
 1994    "How common is workplace transformation and who
         adopts it?" *Industrial and Labor Relations Review* 47:
         173–188.
Ouchi, William
 1981    *Theory Z: How American Business Can Meet the Jap-
         anese Challenge.* New York: Addison-Wesley.
Parnell, Phillip
 1978    "Village or state: competitive legal systems in a Mex-
         ican judicial district." Pages 315–350 in *The Disputing
         Process: Law in Ten Societies*, edited by Laura Nader
         and Harry F. Todd, Jr. New York: Columbia University
         Press.
Parsons, Talcott
 1942    "Propaganda and social control." *Psychiatry* 24:551–
         572.
Paules, Greta Foff
 1991    *Dishing it Out: Power and Resistance among Wait-
         resses in a New Jersey Restaurant.* Philadelphia: Tem-
         ple University Press.
Pilcher, William W.
 1972    *The Portland Longshoremen: A Dispersed Commu-
         nity.* New York: Holt, Rinehart, and Winston.
Piombino, Christine
 1995    Management Consulting as Social Control. Unpub-
         lished Master's Thesis, Department of Sociology, Uni-
         versity of New Hampshire.
Polsky, Andrew J.
 1991    *The Rise of the Therapeutic State* Princeton: Princeton
         University Press.
Poole, Eric D., and R. M. Regoli
 1980    "Race, institutional rule breaking, and discipli-

nary response." *Law and Society Review* 14:931–946.

Powell, Walter W.
1990    "Neither market nor hierarchy: network forms of organization." Pages 295–336 in *Research in Organizational Behavior*, Volume 12, edited by Barry M. Staw and L. L. Cummings. Greenwich, Connecticut: JAI Press.

Rapoport, John D., and Brian L. P. Zevnik
1989    *The Employee Strikes Back!* New York: MacMillian.

Rayman, Paula
1981    *The Kibbutz Community and Nation Building.* Princeton: Princeton University Press.

Reiss, Albert J., Jr.
1971    *The Police and the Public.* New Haven: Yale University Press.

Rice, John Steadman
1996    *A Disease of One's Own: Psychotherapy, Addiction, and the Emergence of Co-Dependency.* New Brunswick: Transaction Publishers.

Rieff, Phillip
1966    *The Triumph of the Therapeutic.* New York: Harper and Row.

Robertson, Constance Noyes (editor)
1970    *Oneida Community: An Autobiography, 1851–1876.* Syracuse: Syracuse University Press.

Robin, Gerald D.
1967    "The corporate and judicial disposition of employee thieves." *Wisconsin Law Review* Summer:685–702.

Roethlisberger, F. J., and William J. Dickson
1939    *Management and the Worker.* Cambridge: Harvard University Press.

Rohlen, Thomas P.
1974    *For Harmony and Strength: Japanese White-Collar Organization in Anthropological Perspective.* Berkeley: University of California Press.

Roman, Paul
1980    "Medicalization and social control in the workplace: prospects for the 1980s." *Journal of Applied Behavioral Science* 16:407–423.

Rosen, Corey, Katherine J. Klein, and Karen M. Young
1986   *Employee Ownership in America*. Lexington: Lexington Books.

Rothlenberger, John E.
1978   "The social dynamics of dispute settlement in a Sunni Muslim village in Lebanon." Pages 152–180 in *The Disputing Process: Law in Ten Societies*, edited by Laura Nader and Harry F. Todd, Jr. New York: Columbia University Press.

Rothschild, Joyce, and J. Allen Whitt
1986   *The Cooperative Workplace: Potentials and Dilemmas of Organizational Democracy and Participation*. New York: Cambridge University Press.

Rothschild-Whitt, Joyce
1979   "The collectivist organization: an alternative to bureaucratic models." *American Sociological Review* 44: 509–527.

Roy, Donald
1952   "Quota restriction and goldbricking in a machine shop." *American Journal of Sociology* 57:427–442.

Russell, Raymond
1985   *Sharing Ownership in the Workplace*. Albany: State University of New York Press.

Scheff, Thomas
1961   "Control over policy by attendants in a mental hospital." *Journal of Health and Social Behavior* 2:93–101.
1966   *Becoming Mentally Ill*. Hawthorne, N.Y.: Aldine.

Scott, William G.
1965   *The Management of Conflict: Appeal Systems in Organizations*. Homewood, Illinois: Irwin-Dorsey.

Scull, Andrew
1989   *Social Order/Mental Disorder: Anglo-American Psychiatry in Historical Perspective*. Berkeley: University of California Press.

Selznick, Philip
1969   *Law, Society, and Industrial Justice*. New York: Russell Sage.

Senechal de la Roche, Roberta
1996   "Collective violence as social control." *Sociological Forum* 11:971–28.

1997    "The sociogenesis of lynching." Pages 48–76 in *Under Sentence of Death: Lynching in the South,* edited by W. Fitzhugh Brundage. Chapel Hill: University of North Carolina Press.

Serron, Carroll

1988    "The professional project of parajudges: the case of U.S. magistrates." *Law and Society Review* 22:557–574.

Shorter Edward, and Charles Tilly

1974    *Strikes in France, 1830–1968.* London: Cambridge University Press.

Silberman, Matthew

1985    *The Civil Justice Process: A Detroit Area Study.* Orlando: Academic Press.

Silbey, Susan S., and Sally Engle Merry

1986    "Mediator settlement strategies." *Law and Policy* 8:7–32.

Simon, Herbert

1976    *Administrative Behavior.* New York: Free Press (third edition).

Simpson, Richard L.

1985    "Social control of occupations and work." *Annual Review of Sociology* 11:415–436.

Skolnick, Jerome

1966    *Justice without Trial: Law Enforcement in Democratic Society.* New York: John Wiley.

Smith, M. Dwayne

1987    "Patterns of discrimination in assessments of the death penalty: the case of Louisiana." *Journal of Criminal Justice* 15:279–286.

Smith, Vicki

1990    *Managing in the Corporate Interest: Control and Resistance in an American Bank.* Berkeley: University of California Press.

Snowden, Frank M.

1986    *Violence and Great Estates in the South of Italy: Apulia. 1900–1922.* Cambridge: Cambridge University Press.

Spiro, Melford E.

1956    *Kibbutz: Adventure in Utopia.* New York: Shocken Books.

Starr, June
1978    "Turkish village disputing behavior." Pages 122–151
        in *The Disputing Process: Law in Ten Societies*, edited
        by Laura Nader and Harry F. Todd, Jr. New York: Co-
        lumbia University Press.
Sudnow, David
1965    "Normal crimes: sociological features of the penal
        code in a public defender's office." *Social Problems*
        12:255–276.
Szasz, Thomas S.
1961    *The Myth of Mental Illness: The Foundations of a The-
        ory of Personal Conduct.* New York: Harper.
1994    *Cruel Compassion: Psychiatric Control of Society's
        Unwanted.* New York: John Wiley and Sons.
Tannenbaum, Arnold S.
1968    *Control in Organization.* New York: McGraw-Hill.
Todd, Harry F., Jr.
1978    "Litigious marginals: character and disputing in a Ba-
        varian village." Pages 86–121 in *The Disputing Process:
        Law in Ten Societies*, edited by Laura Nader and Harry
        F. Todd, Jr. New York: Columbia University Press.
Toscano, David J.
1983    *Property and Participation: Employee Ownership and
        Workplace Democracy in Three New England Firms.*
        New York: Irvington Publishers.
Trice, Harrison M. and William J. Sonnenstuhl
1990    "Alcohol and mental health programs in the work-
        place." *Research in Community and Mental Health*
        6:351–378.
Trubeck, David M., Joel B. Grossman, William L. F. Felstiner,
Herbert M. Kritzer, and Austin Sarat
1983    *Civil Litigation Research Project: Final Report.* Part A.
        Madison: University of Wisconsin Law School.
Tucker, James
1989    "Employee theft as social control." *Deviant Behavior*
        10:319–334.
1993    "Everyday forms of employee resistance." *Sociologi-
        cal Forum* 8:25–45.
Tucker, James, and Susan Ross
1999    "Corporal punishment and Black's theory of social

control." Forthcoming in *Corporal Punishment in Theoretical Perspective*, edited by Michael J. Donnelly and Murray A. Straus. New Haven: Yale University Press.

United States Bureau of Census
   1975   *Historical Statistics of the United States.*

United States Department of Labor (Bureau of Labor Statistics)
   1996   *Employment and Earnings*, Volume 43.

Van Maanen, John
   1992   "Drinking our troubles away: managing conflict in a British Police Agency." Pages 32–62 in *Hidden Conflict in Organizations: Uncovering Behind-the-Scenes Disputes*, edited by Deborah M. Kolb and Jean M. Bartunek. Newbury Park: Sage.

van Onselen, Charles
   1976   *Chibaro: African Mine Labour in Southern Rhodesia, 1900–1933.* Johannesburg: Raven Press.

Wanner, Craig
   1975   "The public ordering of private relations. Part one: initiating civil cases in urban trial courts." *Law and Society Review* 8:421–440.
   1976   "The public ordering of private relations. Part two: winning civil court cases." *Law and Society Review* 9: 293–306.

Weber, Max
   1925   *Max Weber on Law in Economy and Society*, edited by Max Rhenstein. Cambridge: Harvard University Press.

Weiss, Richard M.
   1986   *Managerial Ideology and the Social Control of Deviance in Organizations.* New York: Praeger Publishers.

Westin, Alan F., and Alfred G. Feliu
   1988   *Resolving Employment Disputes without Litigation.* Washington, D.C.: Bureau of National Affairs.

Whyte, William F.
   1948   *Human Relations in the Restaurant Industry.* New York: McGraw-Hill.
   1988   *Making Mondragon: The Growth and Dynamics of the Worker Cooperative Complex.* Ithaca: ILR Press.

Wilson, James Q.
  1968  *Varieties of Police Behavior: The Management of Law
         and Order in Eight Communities.* Cambridge: Harvard
         University Press.
Yngvesson, Barbara
  1988  "Making law at the doorway: the clerk, the court, and
         the construction of community in a New England
         town." *Law and Society Review* 22:409–448.
Yngvesson, Barbara, and Patricia Hennessey
  1975  "Small claims, complex disputes: a review of the
         small claims literature." *Law and Society Review* 9:
         219–274.
Zablocki, Benjamin
  1971  *The Joyful Community.* Baltimore: Penguin.
Zwerdling, Daniel
  1978  *Workplace Democracy.* New York: Harper and Row.

# Index